BECOMING THE NOBLE WOMAN

by Anita Young

HENSLEY
PUBLISHING
Tulsa, Oklahoma

ACKNOWLEDGMENTS

The author wishes to express thanks to Pastor David Schwambach who helped birth the idea of Noble Women, and to his wife, Kris Schwambach, who helped birth the idea of my becoming a writer. My thanks to Cindy Larrison and "Missionary Mary" for being a role model of a Noble Woman for me and to my two disciples, Nina Paolo and Sherry Palmer, who have learned what it means to be Noble Women. And all my gratitude to my precious husband, Gary, who over the years has told me "Many women do noble things but you surpass them all." (Proverb 31:29)

The Bible Version used in this book, unless otherwise noted, is the New International Version.

ABOUT THE AUTHOR

When Anita Young is not teaching a Christian education class, she is writing material for one. Within the 20 churches where her husband has ministered, she has taught young married couples, directed primary church and Babyland Nursery, taught Sunday School classes from age 5 to adult, and led home Bible studies for women. Out of these home studies came the idea for BECOMING THE NOBLE WOMAN. Anita has been teaching this course for 10 years.

Sue has taught kindergarten and preschool chapel for Trinity Education Center in San Antonio, Texas. In addition, she wrote and coordinated a daily Bible curriculum for the preschool.

Anita has also written and published articles, devotionals and Sunday School material. She and her husband, Gary, have three children — Jeremy, Sarah and Leah.

TABLE OF CONTENTS

I Proverbs 31

II Wisdom

III Stature

I-1

Lesson 1
Proverbs 31

PURPOSE
To discover God's purpose and desires for a Christian woman.

OVERVIEW
Proverbs 31:10-31 was taught to young Jewish girls as a means of teaching them the qualities and character God expected them to exhibit as a woman and wife. The "Noble Woman" has been esteemed by scholars as God's ideal woman.

Because of this, these verses are a blueprint for you as a woman to follow to become the best Christian and the best woman possible for God.

DISCUSSION
Verse by Verse Study.

Read verses 10-31 one at a time. Notes follow each verse. Allow for discussion of each quality. Note modern equivalents where applicable.

Vs. 10: *"A wife of noble character who can find? She is worth far more than rubies."* She's **valuable.** The definition for noble is "excellent." We're discussing the excellent woman. She's worth far more than rubies. The choice of rubies is interesting. A ruby is the purest gem.

Vs. 11: *"Her husband has full confidence in her and lacks nothing of value."* She's **trustworthy.** Her husband, or for that matter anyone close to her, can rest assured she won't spill any secrets, tattle any tales, or reveal her husband in a bad light to anyone (especially her mother or mother-in-law!). This is a valuable commodity to a husband and one that will be rewarded with more and more confidences.

Vs. 12: *"She brings him good, not harm, all the days of her life."* She is **beneficial.** She adds to the joy and fullness of her husband's life; she doesn't detract from that joy and fullness in any way.

Vs. 13: *"She selects wool and flax and works with eager hands."* She's **caring.** She takes time to select the best materials for her

1

work. She has an enthusiastic interest in making things for her family.

Vs. 14: *"She's like the merchant ships, bringing her food from afar."* She's **giving.** She goes the extra mile to provide for her husband and children's needs. Merchant ships traveled long and hazardous journeys to bring new, exciting, pleasurable, and valuable commodities back home.

Vs. 15: *"She gets up while it is still dark; she provides food for her family and portions for her servant girls."* She's **administrative.** She's the first one up in the household to insure the day starts right. She takes care of the needs of her family and those under her authority. She's disciplined.

Vs. 16: *"She considers a field and buys it; out of her earnings she plants a vineyard."* She's an **entrepreneur.** She knows how to earn and manage money for a greater return. This is the first of many contacts in the business world. She has time in her life to be enterprising in business. This woman has discovered her many talents. You don't have to have the identical talents, sewing, gardening, trading, and probably cooking, that this woman did, but you should use your talents (or learn new ones) to benefit your family and bring yourself pleasure.

Vs. 17: *"She sets about her work vigorously, her arms are strong for her tasks."* She's **strong.** This woman has energy enough for her busy day. The secret of her bountiful source of energy is found in verses 15, 25, 27, and 30. She's organized, doesn't burden herself with worry, keeps her schedule full, and submits herself to the Lord.

Vs. 18: *"She sees that her trading is profitable, and her lamp does not go out at night."* She has business sense and is a **hard worker.** This woman is tops in getting the most money for her goods and the most goods for her money (today's refunding champion?). She's willing to put in long hours to get the job done right.

Vs. 19: *"In her hand she holds the distaff and grasps the spindle with her fingers."* She has a **talent.** She takes the carefully selected wool from verse 13 and begins to turn it into garments for her family and business.

Vs. 20: *"She opens her arms to the poor and extends her hands to the needy."* She's **compassionate.** A Christian woman should have time set aside for the needs of the Body of Christ. Jesus instructed us to give to the needy in His name, to take care of widows and fatherless children, to visit the sick and those in prison, and to teach young men and women. A woman isn't exempt from these commands of the Lord.

Vs. 21: *"When it snows, she has no fear for her household; for all of them are clothed in scarlet."* She's **wise.** The fear of the Lord is the beginning of wisdom. She shows wisdom by not being afraid of the future. She isn't anxious over the winter approaching. She trusts God to take care of their increased needs during cold weather. (Scarlet material in that day was the heavier wool worn in winter. This woman made sure her family had warm clothes for the winter.)

Vs. 22: *"She makes coverings for her bed; she is clothed in fine linen and purple."* She's **classy.** A Noble Woman doesn't neglect herself or ignore her own tastes. Fine linen and purple were the expensive, designer materials of that day. This woman wore nice, beautiful clothes of good quality and displayed her personal decorator's touch in her bedroom.

Vs. 23: *"Her husband is respected at the city gate, where he takes his seat among the elders of the land."* She's proud and **supportive** of her husband. The city gate is where the elders of the city sat and discussed important issues of commerce, justice, and government. Part of a man's respect comes out of his own self-worth and confidence, which can be nurtured initially and primarily by his wife. The Noble Woman's husband is respected in part because of her encouragement. She can have joy in taking a portion of the credit for his accomplishments. The importance of the position of supportive member to another's fruit is not to be viewed lightly. In a similar way, the Holy Sprit is the support behind all that Jesus did on earth. We don't consider the Holy Spirit to be any less than God the Father or God the Son.

Vs. 24: *"She makes linen garments and sells them, and supplies the merchants with sashes."* She's **industrious** and a financial additive to the home. This woman worked out of her home and oversaw the entire production of undergarments and money purses from choosing the flax, to spinning it into thread, sewing it, and selling it herself. The word "supplies" may also indicate that in addition to selling, she bartered or traded (see verse 18).

Vs. 25: *"She is clothed with strength and dignity; she can laugh at the days to come."* She has **inward beauty** and a carefree attitude toward life. She has the dignity of knowing her self-worth regardless of her youth or outward appearance. She can laugh at growing old, not worried about showing wrinkles or other signs of age. She trusts God to take care of the future.

Vs. 26: *"She speaks with wisdom, and faithful instruction is on her tongue."* She's a **teacher.** This could include teaching children, servants, the poor, and merchants, with works of wisdom.

Vs. 27: *"She watches over the affairs of her household and does not eat the bread of idleness."* She's administrative, organized, and a **hard worker.** She keeps on top of her household and family situation even though she's occupied in business and social endeavors as well. Most modern women realize it doesn't take 24 hours a day to oversee an organized, efficient household once children are occupied in school. Even without today's timesaving devices, the Noble Woman delegated work to servants. Idleness is a grave disease which leads to depression, laziness, gossip, and little produced fruit. The Noble Woman's example is to find the right mixture of household duties, community service, and business ventures to make the day busy and fulfilling.

Vs. 28: *"Her children arise and call her blessed; her husband also, and he praises her."* She's **rewarded** for her labors. Beginning with this verse we see the fruit and rich harvest this woman receives by being so sensitive to the needs of her family. Her children, as they age, bless her (bring her great joy) with their words. They think she's wonderful and aren't ashamed of her. Her husband, in addition, praises her for all her help to him and their children and for the witness for God she has been to others. She hears the best compliment any husband could tell his wife, "You are the most excellent woman I know." What love and devotion goes behind those words. Every husband could honestly say this to **his** wife, for only **she** can be the most excellent woman in meeting his needs.

Vs. 29: *"Many women do noble things, but you surpass them all."* Her husband praises her for her excellent virtue in all she does.

Vs. 30: *"Charm is deceptive, and beauty is fleeting; but a woman who fears the Lord is to be praised."* The Noble Woman **receives** praise from God. He doesn't look on the outward appearance of charm and beauty, but on her heart and how much she fears Him, with awe and respect, for His Lordship over her life.

Vs. 31: *"Give her the reward she has earned, and let her works bring her praise at the city gate."* She **receives** her reward and praise from the community. Social recognition of a job well done was given at the city gate. It's no coincidence this was where her husband worked. They not only shared a oneness at home, but also in the marketplace. In other words, a husband can also take credit for his wife's accomplishments (as she did for his in verse 23). They aren't in competition with each other, but are an extension of each other.

SUMMARY

This woman, on first glance, appears perfect and too ideal to be real. She's the epitome of superwife, supermom, and superbusinesswoman. You must realize this is a backward glance of a woman's entire life. She didn't do all these things in one day, or even one year. No one can get up while it's still dark and not let her lamp go out at night for very long without losing her effectiveness. The secret this woman possessed was the wisdom to know when to get up before dawn and when to work through the night so she never lost her effectiveness. Her goals were clear and her motives were pure. She knew what her talents were and used them for everyone's benefit. She wasn't afraid of working with the business world but also supported her husband's work. She wasn't afraid of change or trying a new venture. She assumed the responsibilities of a Godly woman by teaching and giving, from her own hands to the poor. She didn't produce all these qualities, talents, and business deals overnight but let God develop them within her, waiting for the appropriate opportunities to go where God led her.

This, then, is achievable by every Christian woman. It is something you can learn to achieve now, and thus, call yourself a Noble Woman.

ASSIGNMENT

To begin being a Noble Woman, you must realize your power comes from Jesus Christ. You're dead to yourself and alive unto God. You may think you possess none of the qualities of a Noble Woman, but Jesus, within you, possesses them all. The study of

Romans 6 will help you believe and claim this first step in being a Noble Woman. You'll be memorizing all of Romans 6. This isn't as great a feat as you might think. As you memorize six verses each week you will see how one verse flows into another like a beautiful poem. The constant repetition will get down into your spirit until the words flow from the heart and you have no difficulty understanding that Christ within you can do and be all you desire. This week, memorize Romans 6:1-6.

Suggestion: Memorize one verse at a time, breaking the verse into phrases. Work for accuracy, reading a phrase and repeating the phrase from memory until every word is correct. You might prefer memorizing in the King James Version since the language is lyrical and poetic, making it easier to recall from memory.

I-1

TABLE 1
PROVERBS 31

QUALITY	VERSE
Valuable	10-31
Pure	10
Trustworthy	11
Beneficial	12, 16, 18, 24, 28
Talented	13, 16, 18, 22, 24, 28
Caring	13, 15, 21
Thrifty	13, 18
Giving	14, 20
Organized	15, 16, 21, 27
Administrative	15, 16, 27
Enterprising	16, 18, 24
Strong, Hard Worker	17, 18, 27
Compassionate	20
Wise	21, 25, 26
Classy	22
Supportive	23
Inward Beauty	25
Honest Humility	28, 30, 31

Lesson 2
Self-Evaluation A

I-2

PURPOSE

To learn that many women do noble things, but you can surpass them all.

OVERVIEW

The Noble Woman evaluations are divided into five sections to correspond with the five categories in this program. The first evaluation corresponds with the study in Lesson 1 about the Noble Woman discussed in Proverbs 31. These questions are designed to help you gain a clear image of who the Noble Woman was and apply your own qualities to those of the Noble Woman. Questions are to be answered for your personal use, so be as honest with yourself as you can concerning your walk with the Lord and your desires. This self-examination is to help organize your life into the five categories studied in this Bible course, and to identify strengths and weaknesses you have in the different categories and areas of growth. Once pinpointed, you can bring your strengths into submission to God and turn your weaknesses into new strengths by learning God's principles and methods for growing in these areas. The questions will help you discover your new awareness as to who the Noble Woman was and how you personally can fit into that image. After answering the questions, discuss your answers with the class openly to help each other to become Noble Women.

SELF-EVALUATION

1. What qualities does a Noble Woman have? What qualities did we discuss in Lesson 1 in reading over the verses in Proverbs 31? Try to answer this question from memory so that those qualities which stand out most in your mind will have priority. This will give you a clue to the qualities you most admire about the Noble Woman. We listed 17 qualities for the Noble Woman; many of them could be named in different ways. List as many as you can. Refer to Lesson 1 if necessary.

_____

_____

_____

_____

_____

_____

_____

_____

_____

_____

_____

2. Which of the qualities do you now possess? Answer this question by listing those qualities you feel are your strong points. Perhaps you have qualities that were not named but would apply as well. Name them. This will give you an idea of how you are already growing into a Noble Woman of God.

_____

_____

_____

_____

_____

_____

_____

_____

_____

3. Describe the Noble Woman's home situation. What kind of activities did she do on a regular basis, inside and outside the home? What were her mornings like? How did she provide for her husband and children? How did she run her household? How did she run her business? What kind of activities did she engage in during evening hours? Try to describe the Noble Woman's entire lifestyle as it revolved around the home she was building for her family.

_____

_____

_____

_____

_____

_____

_____

4. Describe **your** home situation. Remember, the true definition of humility is not to be extremely self-critical but to be truly honest about your gifts as well as weaknesses. What kind of things take up your time? What activities do you do for your husband and children? What kind of talents do you use? What business ventures interest you? In what ways do you meet the needs of others less fortunate than yourself?

I-2

_____

_____

_____

_____

_____

_____

_____

5. List the priorities the Noble Woman had, then list yours beside them. Notice the Noble Woman placed her family above her business ventures. She was always careful to provide for her family's needs. She made sure her husband was able to do his job and received the emotional support he needed at home. She managed the training of her children, yet she also allowed time to use her talents in activities she enjoyed. She had a priority to make a profit when she used her talents in the business world. Review your own life for these, and other priorities, and list them.

_____

_____

_____

_____

_____

_____

_____

_____

6. Where did the Noble Woman receive the power to accomplish all that she did? As you look in verse 30, which says, *"Charm is deceptive, and beauty is fleeting; but a woman who fears the Lord is to be praised,"* you will notice the Noble Woman knew the value of honoring and fearing the Lord. She submitted to Him as Lord and allowed Him to control her life. This way she was strengthened, because the joy of the Lord became her strength. She had purpose in her life and believed God was in control of her circumstances. She was confident she was fulfilling the will of God.

_____

_____

_____

_____

_____

_____

_____

7. After memorizing Romans 6:1-6, who do you realize enables you to be a Noble Woman? Allowing your weaknesses to overshadow your strengths is sin. Did you recognize, while memorizing Romans 6, that in identifying yourself with Jesus, by being a Christian, you have gained His resurrection power to give you new life in all areas of your life? As you're united with Christ in His resurrection, you know that your old self is gone. Anything that would stop you from becoming a Noble Woman is buried and powerless. This is the first step in becoming a Noble Woman.

_____

_____

_____

_____

_____

_____

_____

8. What qualities of a Noble Woman will you commit to acquire in the next year? Although it's difficult to give a time frame for the working of the Holy Spirit, allow plenty of time for God to do His work in your life. God takes time with His people. God works from the inside out, beginning with changing your heart, until gradually, those almost imperceptible changes have affected your manner and behavior. What qualities do you most admire in the Noble Woman? If God has made it possible for one woman to be a Noble Woman, He can also make it possible for you.

I-2

_____

_____

_____

_____

_____

_____

_____

_____

9. What do you think is God's purpose for your life? Many Christians go through their Christian lives with a very vague perception of God's viewpoint of their life. They often feel that God is removed from their everyday life. They believe He's only interested in the most important facets of their life to the exclusion of the ordinary. Nothing could be further from the truth. God is, indeed, interested in every intricate detail of your life. He has a perfect plan to fulfill what He made you at birth. You can blossom into the being He desires you to be. God is, more interested in who you are than what you do. God has a reason for you being in your country, your city, your family, your job, and your church. Determine what God's purpose is for your life, specifically. Whose lives does He want you to touch? In what ways does He want you to serve the body of believers in your local church? How does He want you to be a witness for Him?

_____

_____

_____

_____

_____

_____

_____

10. Do you desire to be a Noble Woman? Why? What are your motives behind your desire to be a Noble Woman? What do you want to accomplish by achieving this growth? How do you feel about the difference between your previous notion of God's ideal woman and what you found the reality to be?

_____

_____

_____

_____

_____

_____

_____

_____

_____

SUMMARY

The Noble Woman in Proverbs 31 had the same concerns as women today—running an efficient household, being a good companion to her husband, giving her children the best start in life, and making her mark in the business world. Nowhere does it say that she had extraordinary beauty or a size 10 figure. Her husband had neither the richest nor the poorest occupation, yet he was regarded admirably in the business world, in part, because of her support. Because of her attitude and care at home, her children grew up to say she was the best mom in the world. She was able to meet all these needs, have a purpose, and fulfill that purpose because of her trust in the Lord. Women today can do the same. **You** can be a Noble Woman and surpass them all.

ASSIGNMENT

Memorize Romans 6:7-12. You'll find many of the verses throughout chapter six are repetitive thoughts. This is so the Christian can achieve a full understanding of victory over sin and negative qualities. You must believe that God can do the work in you. With His help, you can possess the qualities of a Noble Woman. Read Proverbs 31:29 daily and begin the work of a Noble Woman.

Suggestion: Write out your memory verses on 3 x 5 cards. Copy the verses two or three times. The mental exercise of reading and copying puts the words automatically into the beginning of memory. You'll be surprised how much you'll remember when the exercise is done.

Lesson 3
Becoming a Noble Woman

I-3

PURPOSE

To discover the four sides of being a Noble Woman.

OVERVIEW

It isn't so much **what** the Noble Woman did that made her successful as much as **how** she did it all. You've learned the only way to be a Noble Woman is to allow the power of God within you to do the work. Because it's Him and not you, you **can** be a Noble Woman. As you look over the list of the Noble Woman's accomplishments, you see they fall into four areas. These four areas of a balanced life can be likened to the four equal sides of a square. That balance is the foundation for you to build on.

Jesus, the One whom you should pattern your life after, gives you the example to follow in Luke 2:52. He grew mentally, physically, spiritually, and socially, as you must. A Noble Woman should keep each of these four areas of growth in perfect balance. To begin this kind of noble life you need basic principles to make the four sides of the square proportional. This lesson will deal with those principles.

DISCUSSION

Read Luke 2:52, *"And Jesus grew in wisdom and stature, and in favor with God and men."* This is how Jesus grew; He grew in each area. He had balance. He grew mentally (wisdom), physically (stature), spiritually (favor with God), and socially (favor with men). Jesus took time as He grew up to learn about wisdom. He didn't just learn facts, but also learned God's reasonings behind those facts. It was the human side of Jesus that grew in wisdom. He used His mind, will, and emotion to understand God's world; the truths about the workings of nature; the laws of faith, hope and love; and the wise way to live in balance with Himself, God the Father, and other men. Jesus grew in stature as He ate the foods which provided the best fuel for His body. He took care of His body by not getting drunk and by getting enough exercise and sleep. He fasted at least once, for forty days. It's not surprising that Jesus had God's favor, but the Bible said He **grew** in that favor. He did this by spending time with God the Father daily, by submitting always to the Father's will, and by being concerned about matters which concerned the Father. Jesus didn't neglect growing in favor with men. He often took the disciples away to be alone with Him. He shared private thoughts with them and told them new things about Himself and the Father. He took the time to be a true friend to them. You can emulate the life of Jesus and begin to grow in wisdom, stature, and favor with God and men.

Look at the Noble Woman's life. She grew in wisdom by using her mental capabilities according to God's natural and ethical laws. She administrated and organized her life wisely to be productive and submissive to God. She redeemed her time by using her talents and following God's wise laws of giving. Physically, she kept up her appearance and worked hard. She developed qualities of compassion and fear of the Lord, which brought her into favor with God. She didn't neglect others. She grew in favor with her family and community as well. Her characteristics can be divided among the four areas of growth.

MENTAL	PHYSICAL	SPIRITUAL	SOCIAL
Talented	Strong	Pure	Valuable
Thrifty	Hard Worker	Giving	Trustworthy
Organized	Classy	Compassionate	Beneficial
Administrative	Appearance	Inward Beauty	Supportive
Enterprising		Humility	
Wise			

To begin to balance your life, you must start with a strong foundation of basic life principles. These principles are few and simple, but failing to follow them can cause you to stumble through life trying to be noble but always being hopelessly out of balance instead. The principles are interlocking links — leave out one and the chain of support collapses. Get a clear image of the principles—first fruits, redeeming the time, giving, and receiving—and you'll be able to balance the four areas of your growth.

First Fruits

Priorities, priorities, priorities. Learn the art of putting first things first. It's a natural progression of responsibilities, as simple as washing your hands. First you turn on the water, then you get your hands wet. You add the soap, rinse, turn off the water and dry your hands. You can't get wet before you turn on the faucet, or dry until after getting wet. When time is short you might condense it to faucet, rinse, faucet, dry, but the order is the same. You must know the order of your life. God said to put Him first (Matthew 6:33), family second (I Timothy 5:8), then your neighbor (I John 3:17). Give your money (Malachi 3:10), time (Ephesians 5:15-16), talent (I Peter 4:10), and goals (Proverbs 16:3) to God first.

It's interesting that God never mentions putting yourself into the order of priorities except in last place (Matthew 16:24). This is a difficult concept to believe and follow in the ME decade. The world says, "Put yourself first," and "Look out for number 1." God says, "Deny yourself, pick up your cross, and follow me," and "It is better to give than to receive." It's not necessary to work 16-hour days for others until burnout occurs. Even Jesus relaxed with His friends and wanted to be alone sometimes. There's a difference between the pampering going on in the world today and the true times of regeneration the Lord wants you to take for yourself.

Pampering yourself is not assuming responsibilities that may be difficult, taking the easy way out in every situation, or padding your life so you can never grow through adversity. Refreshing yourself is being alone with God, yourself, or friends, for a time of relaxation between times of great responsibility.

Redeeming the Time

This corresponds with first fruits. Redeeming the time involves self-control, self-denial, and a good sense of priorities. You're accountable for every thought, word, and deed (Romans 14:12). You need to be as good a steward of your time as you are with your finances. If you waste your money, you may earn it back; but if you lose time, you can never regain it. An appropriate use of time is a blessing, itself, and a talent to develop. After you know what your priorities (first fruits) are, then you need to know how to take care of them (redeeming the time). God has never given a responsibility without the adequate amount of time needed to accomplish the task.

Time management is a major part of the information service industry right now. People have more responsibilities than ever before and need to know how to get them all done effectively. The Noble Woman, too, had to juggle home, business and, social life with personal time. The point to be made is: You can't do it all at the same time; but there is a way to get it all done. That is, to get all done that the Lord wants done. Most time management books and seminars don't take into consideration that you're a servant of God. You need to do what He wants you to do and not worry about the rest. Most time management involves your obligations to others.

Giving (Discipling)

Jesus was always involved in multiplication. He multiplied food, miracles, and people in His ministry. It's God's plan and purpose for your life to multiply. That means not teaching just one other person in your life to replace yourself, but teaching at least two more. Then those people, in turn, teach others. Having children is an excellent place to start discipling, but raising baby Christians to adult Christians is a faster process. The first Christians began teaching others house to house (Acts 5:42). In Matthew 5:19 Jesus said anyone who taught what He taught would be called great. Even if you're young yourself, you can be teaching others (I Timothy 4:11-12). Your disciple should be younger in the Lord (or at least in the growing process) than you, and treated as a close younger sister. Don't make the mistake of not growing enough in the Lord when you already ought to be teaching others (Hebrews 5:12).

Receiving (Accountability)

God's ways are contrary to what the world teaches. God wants you to give before you receive, not the other way around (Luke 6:38). Once you're giving to someone by discipling them, you need to find a strong Christian woman to be accountable to. Jesus was accountable to His heavenly Father. He did nothing without God's approval. In turn, Jesus' disciples did nothing without Jesus' approval. Paul told the older men to instruct the younger men, and the older women to instruct the younger women (Titus 2:2-8). You should have a Christian woman you can go to with your questions or doubts, prayer burdens and praises. Your relationship with her should be such that she can admonish you, warn you when you aren't working for the Lord's kingdom, encourage you when you're timid to do the will of God, help you when you're weak, and make sure you're kind to everyone. This fulfills the Scripture in I Thessalonians 5:12-15.

Questions
1. What's your purpose in life?
2. How did the Noble Woman in Scripture fulfill her purpose?
3. List the four basic principles of life. Is there any principle you have difficulty accepting or understanding?
4. Using the table at the end of the lesson, write down the characteristics and responsibilities of your life. Are there any imbalances?
5. List the four areas of growth from the area in which you are most developed to least developed.

SUMMARY

As a Christian woman striving to be a Noble Woman, you need to achieve balance within the four sides of your being. In each area of growth you need to let Christ overcome your weakness and be your strength. This is the life of a Noble Woman. She gains wisdom by using her mental capacities to study and apply God's Word to her life and the lives of those she teaches. She develops and disciplines her body physically to have peak performance and energy for the tasks God gives her. She brings all areas under the authority of the Holy Spirit by keeping her spirit attuned to God and developing her relationship with Jesus Christ above all others. She balances these areas with the love of Jesus for others, beginning with her own family, and extending to church and community. Doing this, she is "salt" for the saved, protecting them from the evil one, and "salt" for the unsaved, making them thirsty for God.

ASSIGNMENT

Continue memorizing Romans 6 by adding verses 13-18. By now you can see being a Noble Woman is entirely possible for you, and is desired by God. Pay special attention to verse 17 so you *"obey from the heart that doctrine which was delivered you."* Also read Proverbs 3-5 as you develop the first of the four principles of growth — wisdom. Eventually you will also memorize Proverbs 3. It's a goldmine of wisdom. If you've fallen behind in memorization, determine in your heart now to be fervent in this endeavor. It lays a quick foundation to build upon for being a Noble Woman.

Suggestion: Take the 3 x 5 cards you copied and put them where you know you will glance at them, read them, and perhaps have a few minutes to commit them to memory. Try putting one in the bathroom, in your purse, taped to the dashboard of your car, above your kitchen sink, on your desk, or inside a book you're reading.

TABLE 2
WHOLE PERSON • LUKE 2:52

Luke 2:52 *"And Jesus **grew**." prokopto (Greek) "advance, grow." In the imperfect active tense, "the process goes on."*

I-3

WISDOM
(emotional, mental side)

_____

_____

_____

_____

_____

_____

_____

_____

STATURE
(physical side)

_____

_____

_____

_____

_____

_____

_____

_____

FAVOR WITH MEN
(social side)

_____

_____

_____

_____

_____

_____

_____

_____

FAVOR WITH GOD
(spiritual side)

_____

_____

_____

_____

_____

_____

_____

_____

Lesson 4
Self-Evaluation B

PURPOSE

To discover what you know about wisdom.

OVERVIEW

These questions concern the mental area of growth referred to as wisdom. Take time to think about your answers and write as complete an answer as possible to get a clear understanding of what wisdom is to you, and what your strengths and weaknesses are in this area. Discuss your answers. This could be the beginning of wisdom for some, and a deeper understanding of wisdom for others. Wisdom is necessary in developing all mental abilities (mind, will, and emotion).

SELF-EVALUATION

1. What does wisdom mean to you? Do you ever think about wisdom? It's an elusive quality to most, a mere sign of age-old knowledge to others. Do you have a certain picture in your mind of someone who's wise? What makes him so? Is being wise something you do? Or something you say? Or something you don't do or say? Try to identify wisdom.

_____

_____

_____

_____

_____

_____

_____

_____

_____

_____

_____

2. What Bible verses have you memorized? If you were raised in a Christian home, there are probably certain Bible verses you memorized as a child. Children, who are virtually protected from the evil in the world and still undeveloped in sin nature, are often made to memorize Scripture; while adults, who must battle against principalities and powers (Ephesians 6:12), try to do so without the advantage of Scripture memorization. Have you, as an adult, committed yourself to memorizing Scripture? If so, what types of verses do you memorize?

_____

_____

_____

_____

_____

_____

_____

_____

3. On what principles or words of wisdom do you base your life? People often react to situations in life unconsciously, because of certain thoughts they were programmed to believe in childhood. For instance, if you were taught that "cleanliness is next to Godliness," you might unconsciously feel rejected by God if your house is messy. This phrase, however, isn't even in the Bible. Imagine the change of attitude you might have after realizing you'd believed you must be clean on the **outside** for God to notice the **inside.** Think over your life. What comes to mind when you think of wise words?

_____

_____

_____

_____

_____

_____

_____

_____

_____

4. Explain what you know can be gained with wisdom. Do you believe wisdom is a mental development? What can be gained, then, by having wisdom? What's different about a wise person's life as compared to a regular person's? Does wisdom give you a special ability to live life better or have life treat you better? How can this be? What is it wisdom changes about a person that makes life different from what it would have been without wisdom?

_____

_____

_____

_____

_____

_____

_____

_____

_____

5. Write anything you know the Bible has to say about wisdom. While it's true that the entire Bible is wisdom, which verses can you think of that specifically refer to wisdom? What Bible stories explain wisdom to you? How was Jesus wise? Who else was wise in the Bible? What made them wise? Is wisdom a state of mind or an action, according to these Bible stories and characters? Think over what you know about the Bible. Formulate what you think it says is "wise."

_____

_____

_____

_____

_____

_____

_____

6. How do you overcome bad habits? Bad habits, though not necessarily sin, certainly stem from the fact that you don't submit yourself to God in a certain area and allow the flesh to rule in forcing your mind, will, emotion, and body to repeatedly do something that isn't totally right. *"Let not sin, therefore, reign in your mortal body, that ye should obey it in the lusts therein"* (Romans 6:12). Your body's lust, or dependence on an activity, makes it a habit, whether a chemical reaction which affects your physical side, a belief which affects your mental side, a temptation which affects your spiritual side, or peer pressure which affects your social side. What methods do you use to overcome negative influences on your life?

---

7. Explain different levels of growth you've experienced in the Lord, what the Lord has taught you, and where you now are in your walk with God. How did you come to the Lord? Even if you were raised in a Christian home and church environment, what experience with the Lord affected you in a way that made you want to claim yourself a Christian for life? Once you became a Christian, what did you learn from your Bible, other Christians, or church activities, that made you aware of differences in your old lifestyle and new Christian life? Have you kept learning new things about the Lord and being a Christian? What basic Bible truths have you come to know as a new way of life? How old are you? How long have you been a Christian? Do you see yourself differently than when you first became a Christian? What's your relationship with the Lord right now? In what ways are you trying to develop that relationship? In what areas of your life is God trying to deal with you? These questions will help you see exactly where you are with the Lord in comparison to where you believe you ought to be. They will give you a goal for the years to come.

II-4

_____

_____

_____

_____

_____

_____

_____

_____

8. What's your understanding about the devil, his reason for being, who he is, and his relationship to Christians? When we discuss the life of the Christian and becoming a Noble Woman, you must take into consideration the devil's involvement in your life. Every truth God tries to teach, the devil wants to snatch away or persuade you it's impossible to obey. The devil is merely a fallen angel, not equal to God's almighty power, but he has been given power over this world. *"Put on the full armor of God so that **you** can take your stand against the devil's schemes. For our struggle is not against flesh and blood, but against the rulers, against the authorities, against the powers of this dark world and against the spiritual forces of evil in the heavenly realms"* (Ephesians 6:11-12). Sometimes Christians never feel attacked by the devil. Often it's because they aren't doing the work of God, so the devil doesn't need to bother them. Is the devil attacking you in certain areas? Could it be you're pleasing God and working for His Kingdom and, therefore, have the devil upset with you?

_____

_____

_____

_____

_____

_____

_____

_____

9. Is there something in particular about the devil you don't understand? Have you ever wondered how he stops you from obeying God when you've already been given victory over him

(Romans 6)? Do you have difficulty reading situations in your life, whether it's the devil attacking you or God trying to tell you something? Are you confused about demons and whether or not they can truly possess people? Has the devil been misrepresented by society or the media? You need to know who it is you're fighting against, what powers the devil **actually** has, and what powers he tries to make you **believe** he has. Keep in mind, anything you've heard about the devil from a non-Christian is probably a useful deception and twisted truth. The battleground on which he fights you is your mind. If he can get you to believe certain things about him (such as, his temptations are stronger than the Holy Spirit in you), he has persuaded you toward sin, including the sin of omitting to do God's will. Paul warns often, and Jesus prays as well, for Christians not to be fooled by the devil's tricks. Christians let themselves be tricked into sin. This is why it's important not to be confused about the devil and the ways he attacks. Be aware he'll try to stop you from becoming a Noble Woman.

_____

_____

_____

_____

_____

_____

_____

_____

_____

10. Do you have difficulty knowing God's will in a given situation or doing what you know is His will? Being a Noble Woman means wanting to obey God. But what if you don't know what God's will is? Does God have one perfect outcome for every decision you face? Here again, God isn't interested so much in what you **do** as what you **are.** If you face a decision that isn't one of obeying or disobeying God's Word, but a matter of personal preference (such as whether to buy an economy or luxury car), realize God wants you to have your desires. What He's most concerned with are your motives. Are you trying to obey God with your decision? Do you have peace in your heart concerning your situation? Will your decision cause you to grow farther from God, or closer to Him? If you follow through on this decision, will you have to disobey God? Is there anything about the situation that doesn't seem to follow what the Bible says is a righteous life? The influence of this world is great. Fleshly desires to be upwardly mobile and successful abound. Always question your heart for true motives when making a decision. Ask God what He wants you to do. He never refuses to answer His children when He knows they want to hear Him.

_____
_____
_____
_____
_____
_____
_____
_____
_____
_____

II-4

11. Name some ways you can know God's will. How do you go about determining what God wants you to do when you're faced with a decision? Is there a certain method you follow in seeking God's will? What role do circumstances play in your decision-making? Do you allow emotions to enter into knowing God's will? Do you rely solely on intellect or common sense to guide you in decision making? Or have you conditioned yourself to lay decisions before God in prayer, read His Word for clues of His will, and listen attentively to His still, small voice to hear what He wants you to do. You can determine the growth of a Christian in terms of how much he wants to please God and know God's will concerning every area of his life and every decision he must make.

_____
_____
_____
_____
_____
_____
_____
_____
_____

12. What relationship does the Bible say you have with wisdom? Evaluate exactly what you believe wisdom is, how it affects you, in what ways you are or aren't wise, and what use wisdom can be. What connection do you think you have with wisdom? Are you wise? In what ways? How do you know? How can you

become wiser? In what ways can you change to start being wise? Does wisdom have an important role in your life?

_____

_____

_____

_____

_____

_____

_____

_____

SUMMARY

Obtaining wisdom is highly underrated today. Being wise was once as desirable as good health and financial prosperity. After all, people once believed the adage: "Early to bed and early to rise, makes a man healthy, wealthy, and wise." Today people have replaced wisdom with goal setting, visualization, and other mind tricks that deceitfully convince them they're gaining wisdom. To even begin to have wisdom, you must start by reverencing God (Proverbs 9:10). God has much to say about the normal everyday situations in your life. Most of God's words of wisdom found in the Book of Proverbs deal with attitudes about daily life, and knowing God's will in these situations.

ASSIGNMENT

Continue memorizing Romans 6 by adding verses 18-23. In Proverbs 3-5, you'll read the underlying truths about wisdom that will be discussed in the next lesson. Now read Proverbs 6-8 for additional insights into the many-faceted gem of wisdom.

Suggestion: Practice your memory verses with a partner. One person holds the Bible looking at Romans 6 while the other tries to repeat the verses from memory. The person following in the Bible should stop at **every** mistake during the first recitation and give the correction. After quoting the verses once, the same person recites again. This time overlook minor mistakes.

Lesson 5
The Beginning of Wisdom

II-5

PURPOSE

To learn the advantages of obtaining wisdom. To begin to learn what wisdom is.

OVERVIEW

One definition of wisdom is: "Having good sense." Another is: "Accumulated scientific or philosophic knowledge." George Washington Carver once asked God to show him everything there was to know about the universe. God said, "Your mind isn't big enough." So he asked God to show him everything there was to know about the earth. Again, God said, "Your mind isn't big enough." Finally Carver asked God what his mind **was** big enough to know everything about. God showed him the peanut. The rest, as they say, is history. Wisdom is really God revealing His universe to His children.

Understanding and accepting God's laws, whether they are laws of nature, science, faith, or ethics, is a way to see what God has revealed, and is a sign of growing in wisdom. Knowing the right thing to do or say in any given situation, and having the strength of character to do or say that right thing, is a result of that growth. Your mental side contains not just the mind and emotions but the will as well. You must not only **know** what to do, but **will** yourself to do it. *"What then? Should we continue in sin that grace may abound? God forbid."* When you've learned how to submit your will to God's, from Romans 6, you can grow in the wisdom God reveals about life in the Book of Proverbs.

DISCUSSION

There are some interesting qualities about wisdom as seen in Proverbs 3-7. Wisdom is described as a person, with a distinct personality. No other characteristic of God is described this way. Wisdom is identified in the female gender, as a woman worth far more than rubies. Sound familiar? Is it a coincidence that these are the words used to describe the Noble Woman? This should help you understand why women's intuition is a viable component to the decision-making process. Wisdom is so foundational she was there at the beginning (Proverbs 3:19), in the same way Jesus was there with God (John 1:1).

Wisdom is the female characteristic of Jesus. Wisdom was within Jesus, the second Adam, in the same way Eve was within the first Adam before being taken out of his side. You're to call wisdom your sister, as you call Jesus your brother (Proverbs 7:4).

You learn many things about who wisdom is, and what you'll gain in knowing her, from the Book of Proverbs. Wisdom is the best of the best of possessions, better than silver, rubies, or gold, yet not itself a material possession, but a mental one. (Remember, these comparisons are the closest images the author of Proverbs could relate to in describing wisdom.) Really, nothing can be compared to her in the way of material objects, and nothing totally describes her in the way of mental processes.

Wisdom in Proverbs

The Book of Proverbs is written by King Solomon, whom the Bible considers to be the wisest man in the world. When given a chance to ask God for anything he wanted, Solomon asked for wisdom. The result was a life of great influence, power, wealth, and pleasure. Solomon wanted to pass along the wisdom he'd learned from God to his sons, and thus, wrote the Book of Proverbs. Chapters 3-7 are particularly helpful in understanding the importance of wisdom. Notice below, the number of times you're asked to pay attention to wisdom and acquire it.

Chapter 3

Vs. 7: *"Do not be wise in your own eyes; fear the Lord and shun evil."* If you believe yourself wise because of your own mental capacities, the sin of pride will overtake you.

Vs. 13: *"Blessed is the man who finds wisdom, the man who gains understanding."* Wisdom is something that must be found and gained.

Vs. 21: *"My son, preserve sound judgment and discernment, do not let them out of your sight."* Don't make **any** decisions, no matter how small, without using sound judgment and discerning the Holy Spirit's wishes.

Chapter 4

Vs. 1: *"Listen, my sons, to a father's instruction; pay attention and gain understanding."* When you pay attention to your heavenly Father, you'll gain understanding.

Vs. 4: *"He taught me and said, 'Lay hold of my words with all your heart; keep my commands and you will live.'"* These could be David's words to Solomon, or God's words to David quoted here. Wisdom is a legacy passed from father to son.

Vs. 5: *"Get wisdom, get understanding; do not forget my words or swerve from them."* God's Word is absolute truth; there's no need to look elsewhere for wisdom.

Vs. 7: *"Wisdom is supreme; therefore get wisdom. Though it cost you all you have, get understanding."* God placed the value of wisdom above all mental or material possessions.

Vs. 10: *"Listen, my son, accept what I say, and the years of your life will be many."* Having wisdom is an act of accepting God's will for your life.

Vs. 11: *"I guide you in the way of wisdom and lead you along straight paths."* God is the one to show you wisdom.

Vs. 20: *"My son, pay attention to what I say; listen closely to my words."* Again, God wants you to pay attention.

Chapter 5
Vs. 1: *"My son, pay attention to my wisdom, listen well to my words of insight."* Be sure you hear God's wisdom and not man's.

Chapter 6
Vs. 20: *"My son, keep your father's commands and do not forsake your mother's teaching."* God will reinforce His teaching in your life through the instruction given you by an older Noble Woman.

Vs. 23: *"For these commands are a lamp, this teaching is a light, and the corrections of discipline are the way to life."* Wisdom is synonymous with God's Word. God refers to His Word as a lamp and a light.

Chapter 7
Vs. 1: *"My son, keep my words and store up my commands within you."* Continually storing God's Word brings wisdom.

Vs. 4: *"Say to wisdom, 'You are my sister,' and call understanding your kinsman."* A Noble Woman should strive to develop a relationship with wisdom.

Vs. 24: *"Now then, my sons, listen to me; pay attention to what I say."* At this point, how can anyone refuse to pay attention to what God has to say about wisdom?

II-5

What Wisdom Is Worth
• more profit than silver
• better returns than gold
• more precious than rubies
• nothing compares to her
• any price
• like the first gleam of dawn shining ever brighter
• life and health

How To Get And Produce Wisdom
Getting wisdom from God is as simple as asking Him for it. *"If any of you lacks wisdom, he should ask God, who gives generously to all without finding fault, and it will be given to him"* (James 1:5). What could be an easier way to obtain everything you've ever wanted? The hidden cost, however, is that after getting wisdom (which God will freely give you), you must use wisdom in your decision-making on a regular basis to achieve its rewards. For example, you must:

• use sound judgment
• have discernment
• not withhold good from those who deserve it
• pay for something when you have the money
• not plot harm
• not accuse others
• not envy a violent man

- not be a proud mocker
- be understanding
- lay hold of God's Word
- keep God's commandments
- not forget God's words
- not swerve from God's words
- listen to instruction
- be passive and holy
- follow the path of the righteous
- guard your heart
- put away perverse talk
- fix your gaze directly before you
- consider the path for your feet and take only ways that are firm
- not swerve to the right or the left
- develop insight
- have discretion
- preserve knowledge
- be disciplined
- listen to correction
- obey your teachers
- listen to instructors
- rejoice in your wife (husband)

What Having Wisdom Means

Once you've gained wisdom, many benefits accrue to you. For example, you enjoy:

- riches
- honor
- pleasant ways
- peace
- the tree of life
- blessing
- safety
- no fear
- sweet sleep
- no disaster
- no snare
- a garland of grace
- a crown of splendor
- many years
- unhampered steps
- freedom from stumbling
- life and health for your whole body
- protection from sudden disaster
- protection from the adultress (who destroys, stealing strength and wealth) Note: God refers to many activities as adultery. He said the Jewish race committed adultery when they worshipped idols. Therefore, wisdom can keep you from being tempted and deceived by the cares of this world which could easily become

idols in your life. Such idols are pleasure, career, money, success, etc.

• protection from putting up security for another (the Bible never condones loaning money, only giving money)

II-5

SUMMARY

Who could ask for anything more? Surely we can now better understand why Solomon, when he had a chance to ask God for anything, asked for wisdom. And God was pleased. No one ever disappointed God when asking for wisdom. How exciting to know you have within your grasp the necessary elements to gain anything of value you could possibly want in life by having wisdom. You're to claim her as your sister, and listen to her speak to you (Proverbs 7:4). She stands at the crossroads calling (Proverbs 8:2). Every time you have a decision to make, she's there telling you the right decision. When you ask God for wisdom, and call upon her as your sister, you never have to worry about missing God's will again. As you learn these things and ponder them in your heart, you're growing in wisdom as a Noble Woman.

ASSIGNMENT

Because of the significance of this lesson, the assignment won't involve any memorization. Instead, review and meditate on what you've learned about wisdom. Practice calling to her as your sister in situations where you're discerning God's will. Review what you've memorized in Romans 6. Read and meditate on Philippians 4:8, which can be paraphrased to say, "Think about wisdom."

Suggestion: Meditate on the verse you're trying to memorize. Break the verse into phrases and paraphrase the thought in your own words; then repeat the verse word for word from the Bible. Look up any words you don't know until you're sure exactly what it is you're saying when you quote the Scripture. You'll remember the exact words more easily for they will make more sense.

Lesson 6
How to Grow in Wisdom

II-6

PURPOSE

To see the difference between God's wisdom and man's wisdom.
To become excited about growing in wisdom.

OVERVIEW

Growing in wisdom means not always taking the easy way out. In
Proverbs 8 and Ecclesiastes 7 we learn about wisdom in more
detail. We learn where to find wisdom and what kind of behavior
is exemplified by wisdom. Once you've grown in wisdom, you
need to be aware of lies the devil uses to warp wisdom and keep
you from believing God. The devil is out to steal, kill, and
destroy (John 10:10). One of his most successful campaigns has
been to cloud over the importance of wisdom and what she can
accomplish for you. Learning about the lies of the devil prepares
you for his tricks so you won't be duped into thinking foolishness
is wisdom. The devil does whatever he can to keep you from
learning and using God's truths. The wisdom of man is also
foolishness to God. His ways are above man's ways. Wisdom isn't
a pathway of quick answers, but a lifestyle with long-range
benefits.

DISCUSSION

Read through Proverbs 8 and Ecclesiastes 7. Then discuss the notes.

Proverbs 8

Vs. 1: *"Does not wisdom call out? Does not understanding raise her
voice?"* God doesn't want you to forsake wisdom. He even goes so
far as to have the voice of wisdom call after you. God makes
every way possible for Christians to do the right things and for
women to become Noble Women.

Vs. 4: *"To you, O men, I call out; I raise my voice to all mankind."*
Notice wisdom is available to **all.** God gives wisdom as a gift to
help you achieve everything you want in life.

Vs. 6: *"Listen, for I have worthy things to say; I open my lips to
speak what is right."* As a Christian you should be actively trying
to grow in wisdom; it's a worthy virtue to have. Wisdom tells you
what's right when the devil tries to deceive you.

Vs. 10: *"Choose my instruction instead of silver, knowledge rather
than choice gold."* Here God lets you know that as a Christian you
shouldn't make decisions based on obtaining money. Wisdom is a
better commodity than money since it cannot be stolen,
devalued, or lost.

Vs. 17: *"I love those who love me, and those who seek me find me."* The desire for wisdom is all it takes to obtain wisdom. God made it easy; you only need to seek it.

Vs. 22: *"The Lord possessed me at the beginning of his work, before his deeds of old."* Wisdom is a part of Jesus, therefore, a part of God Himself. How privileged, the Christian, to possess a quality belonging to God.

Vs. 32: *"Now then, my sons, listen to me; blessed are those who keep my ways."* If you've ever asked God to bless you, here's a way to get what you asked for; listen to wisdom and she'll bless you.

Vs. 35: *"For whoever finds me finds life and receives favor from the Lord."* Having wisdom is having life itself.

Ecclesiastes 7

Vs. 8: *"The end of a matter is better than its beginning, and patience is better than pride."* Wisdom is being able to go through situations in your life, have the patience to finish pursuits, and not have pride about your accomplishments.

Vs. 12: *"Wisdom is a shelter as money is a shelter, but the advantage of knowledge is this: that wisdom preserves the life of its possessor."* With wisdom comes a multitude of benefits, not the least of which is a long life. Wisdom tells you how to live the fullest and longest life.

Vs. 18: *"It is good to grasp the one and not let go of the other. The man who fears God will avoid all extremes."* This is the key of the Noble Woman's life; **balance** all four areas of growth.

Vs. 24: *"Whatever wisdom may be, it is far off and most profound who can discover it?"* It can appear complex and just out of grasp, but thanks to Jesus Christ you now have full access to wisdom.

Vs. 27: *"'Look,' says the Teacher, 'this is what I have discovered: Adding one thing to another to discover the scheme of things...'"* This is the pursuit of the Noble Woman. By studying the four areas of growth and trying to achieve balance in these areas, you're adding one thing to another and, thus, gain wisdom.

Ecclesiastes 8

Vs. 1: *"Who is like the wise man? Who knows the explanation of things? Wisdom brightens a man's face and changes its hard appearance."* Gaining wisdom brings great joy. When you're wise, you know you're pleasing God. When you act wisely, you bring great rewards into your life. When you're wise, you're a wonderful friend.

Vs. 5-6: *"The wise heart will know the proper time and procedure. For there is a proper time and procedure for every matter."* This is the Biblical definition of wisdom. As a Noble Woman growing in wisdom, develop the knowledge of the proper time and procedure for everything in your life.

Where to Find Wisdom:

1. **On the mountain top.** When you have a mountain-top

experience, wisdom is there. Usually a mountain comes after a valley. Wisdom, as we see more and more through Proverbs, is the attitude one has through a trial or valley, the ability to thank and praise God despite the situation. This leads to the exhilaration of the mountain top, being "high" on God.

2. **Where two paths meet.** When you come to a crossroads and must make a decision, wisdom is there calling. God is always faithful to communicate His will to you. It's up to you to listen. Realize wisdom is there pointing the direction God wants you to go, even when it's a choice between "better" and "best."

3. **At the gates to the city.** As you saw in Proverbs 31, the elders of the city gathered at the city gates for social, business, and judicial reasons. Every time you meet people in your life and make contact with the outside world, wisdom is there to guide you.

4. **Where there is prudence, knowledge, and discretion.** Many times in the pursuit of knowldge, wisdom is left behind as an anacronism. Wisdom is there waiting when you learn any kind of information, religious or secular. Knowledge has often been called amoral — it can be used for good or evil purposes — but God designed it to be intuitively used for good. God originally intended man to listen and learn from wisdom when he listens and learns from knowledge. Only in the fallen state has man separated the two.

5. **Where Jesus is.** Wisdom is merely a part of the wonderful person of Jesus, in Whom the fullness of the Godhead dwells bodily (Colossians 2:9). This study on wisdom, naming her as a person and even, boldly, as the female side of mankind represented by Jesus, is in no way meant to detract from the fact that when you have Jesus within you, you have everything you'll ever need to be complete. Jesus is the answer to being a Noble Woman; but in identifying wisdom we see Jesus.

Behavior Exemplified by Wisdom:

1. **A good name.** A good reputation can take years to build and only minutes to destroy. In an age where words on paper carry more weight than the spoken word, Christians should strive to be true to their spoken word. A good name is the reward for being accountable for every word you speak.

2. **Full knowledge of death.** A wise person believes in his salvation. He doesn't fear dying, trusts God will take him at the right time, and knows his death is precious in the sight of the Lord (Psalm 116:15).

3. **Mourning and sorrow.** Wisdom isn't just made up of the joys of righteous living; it also includes understanding the sorrows and losses suffered by loved ones. One who truly loves others will feel their losses keenly. Knowing how to accept and walk through grief is a true virtue and sign of wisdom.

4. **Heeding a wise man's rebuke.** The Bible has much to say about discipline (as opposed to punishment). Discipline is the hard training necessary to accomplish a difficult feat. Discipline is something a loving father (and certainly our Heavenly Father)

II-6

is careful to give his child so the child can live a righteous life. A rebuke is a form of discipline. It should be accepted gracefully.

5. **Ending a matter.** In today's world we are caught up with beginnings. We're exhilarated when we begin a family, a career, a marriage, a school, a business project, or even a book. We're often sad when some of these things come to an end. You should look at things in God's light. The accomplishment of raising a family, a celebration at the end of a good life or a finished project is better, in God's eyes, than were their beginnings. God treasures a job well done. Don't leave things unfinished in your life.

6. **Not being quickly provoked.** People can hurt you every day, either intentionally or unintentionally. The devil uses hurt feelings as a foothold to keep you from forgiving, loving, and fellowshipping with the person who hurt you. Striking back in anger only worsens the situation.

7. **Not looking back.** "Why were the 'good old days' better?" This attitude puts up a resistance to change. It also makes you discontent with your present situation and, in a way, blames God for making things worse than they were in the "good old days." Memories are often faulty and paint a rose-colored picture of the past. What a waste of time and energy to view the present in comparison to the past.

8. **Being happy** in good times and considering the bad times. Some people can never be satisfied. When things are going well, they're worried that things will change for the worse. You should enjoy good times without worrying, and consider bad times as growing experiences.

9. **Keeping things in proper perspective.** Don't pay attention to every word people say. First, people don't mean everything they say. (Have you ever said, "Go jump in a lake!") Second, we don't always understand the exact meaning people have for what they say. Third, most people haven't learned to guard their tongues as James warns. It's wise to realize a foolish man will say foolish things which should be disregarded. An uninformed man will say things he knows nothing about. They have no value. People will speak lies, half-truths, ignorant opinions, and hopes of vain glory which don't need to be dignified with a reply.

Lies the Devil Tells:

1. **God won't fulfill His promises.** As soon as you stand on God's Word, the devil is there to refute it. You must not be surprised when this happens; that's his job — to accuse the elect. The devil is inexhaustible in his efforts to dissuade people. He can concentrate on denying God's truth because he has nothing to loose. He knows he's wrong and God is right. He'll take every chance to stand against you because he can't lose any more than he already has.

2. **He's God's equal.** Satan's powers are **not** equal to God's. The devil is a created being, an archangel fallen from grace. The power of evil is less than, not equal to, the power of God.

3. **What harm can it do?** He'll tell you that falling for a

temptation just once won't affect you in the long run. He tries to make sin insignificant in your life. It's often little sins (like procrastination) that so easily beset us (Hebrews 12:13).

4. **That doesn't include you.** He tells you what you read in the Bible couldn't possibly be meant for you. Do you really believe you can do **anything** with God (Philippians 4:13)?

5. **Go with your feelings.** The devil plays on emotions. Anyone who has learned the difference between infatuation and love knows how deceptive emotions can be. People think they're in love when they're in "lust." The devil uses feelings against you by making you **feel** and **think** you're defeated. In reality Jesus won the victory on the cross when He said, "It is finished." Don't believe feelings of defeat. They're a poor standard on which to base decisions.

SUMMARY

Wisdom is expressed throughout the Bible. How wonderful to do all these wise things. Wisdom is a pathway for the Noble Woman to follow to achieve success in all four areas of growth. Don't let the devil persuade you into thinking you can't be wise or can't be a Noble Woman. Instead, believe what God says in Philippians 4:13.

ASSIGNMENT

Begin to memorize Proverbs 3. Meditate on it and hide it in your heart. This chapter has the Bible's most complete expression of wisdom. From now on you should be able to hear wisdom call as you repeat these words daily. This week memorize Proverbs 3:1-3.

Suggestion: Review, review, review. The reason you've never forgotten particular advertising slogans even after commercials are long off the air, is their constant repetition. Hearing a phrase several times until it's memorized, then still hearing it again and again is the secret advertisers know will keep their products in your mind. The same principle can be applied to Bible memorization. Now that you have Romans 6 memorized, don't put it aside thinking you'll never have to read that chapter again. Just reading over the familiar words again will keep them from fading from your memory. You've worked hard to memorize an entire chapter. Don't lose it through neglect.

II-6

TABLE 3

WHERE IS WISDOM IN YOUR LIFE?

1. Are you having a mountain-top experience?

2. Are you facing a decision (large or small) in your life?

3. Are you meeting people in social, business, or legal situations?

4. Are you involved in a correspondence course, seminar, conference, school session, or class of any kind?

5. Are you experiencing a daily relationship with Jesus Christ?

IF YOU ANSWERED YES TO ANY OF THESE QUESTIONS

WISDOM
IS
THERE

Lesson 7
Self-Evaluation C

PURPOSE

To discover the strengths and weaknesses in your physical side and begin to balance this area with wisdom.

OVERVIEW

Your body is a temple for the Holy Spirit (I Corinthians 3:16). Every Christian should want to have that temple in the best of health. Many, however, through neglect, lifestyle, or bad habits have less than optimum health and need to rebuild their temple for the Lord. In **your** efforts to rebuild the temple you shouldn't be interested in a sleek and trim appearance, or how high up the physical fitness ladder you can climb. What you're concerned with is the Christian perspective of your physical nature — how to discipline it and bring it under submission to God. This area of growth needs to be in balance with the others. By taking Noble Woman Self-Evaluation C you'll realize the importance of discipline and submission in this area.

SELF-EVALUATION C

1. Are there eating habits you believe the Lord would have you change? Many Christians don't think the Lord is concerned with the way they treat their bodies. Women on the dieting treadmill are deceived into believing below normal weight is advantageous in life. Eating habits developed over the years can put a barrier between you and God. This is another area God wants you to submit to Him. He has already promised you can overcome any bad habit (Romans 6). What is one particular eating habit you want to start or stop? Be specific about ways you think you can change to become a better servant of God. Are there eating habits you're already aware you're not following because you've been lazy or unwilling to give up old pleasures? Do you need to learn more about nutrition?

_____

_____

_____

_____

_____

_____

_____

_____

_____

_____

2. How much sleep do you need to be your best throughout the day? Sleep should be another area of concern for a Christian. Too often, stress from the job or the many problems of today's society can keep you from falling asleep easily at night or cause your sleep to be fitful. Some housewives have difficulty getting up in the morning to face their day. Some use sleep as an escape from problems and sleep too much for their body's needs. Others shortchange themselves by indulging in late night activities that produce little fruit for God and rob the body of needed sleep.

_____

_____

_____

_____

_____

_____

_____

_____

_____

_____

3. Do you have regular sleeping habits? Why is it adults insist children keep sensible sleep habits and solid routines at bedtime and themselves ignore these same basic rules for lifelong benefits of good health? Setting your body's inner clock to regular sleeping and rising times can be beneficial. It helps your body signal itself to fall asleep quickly so you'll be ready for the next day's duties.

_____

_____

_____

_____

_____

_____

_____

_____

_____

III-7

4. Do you have trouble sleeping or falling asleep? The reason you may have trouble sleeping could be a lack of proper sleeping habits. Try to identify exactly what your problem is so you can ask God to correct it. Are you carrying burdens and prayer concerns without letting God handle them? Are you eating properly and working hard enough throughout the day? Are you at peace with God and with friends and family? Problems in any of the four areas of growth could keep you from sleeping or falling asleep at night.

_____

_____

_____

_____

_____

_____

_____

_____

5. Are there exercise habits you think the Lord would have you change? Exercise is another requirement for optimum health. Have you made room in your life for some form of exercise? Do you engage in any physical activities that include friends? Is **too much** of your time taken up trying to reach an unrealistic weight goal? Are you robbing friends and family of time with you by pursuing an ideal of physical fitness? In what ways would God have you bring your exercise time into better balance?

_____

_____

_____

_____

_____

_____

_____

_____

_____

6. How many hours of exercise do you think you need each week? Each body has its own maximum potential. Part of growing in stature means understanding your own personal exercise needs. As a Noble Woman, you should be at a health level that permits you to comfortably walk briskly through your day; not to experience slumps of depression throughout the day ; accomplish most of what you set out to do (barring interruptions) by working hard, and be sufficiently tired, by day's end, to get an appropriate night's sleep. How much regulated exercise does it take you, weekly, to achieve this daily standard?

_____

_____

_____

_____

_____

_____

_____

_____

_____

7. Explain fasting, its significance and purpose for Christians, and for you in particular. Fasting, as the Bible explains it, is abstention from food for the purpose of drawing closer to God and following His will. This can be done as a partial fast (water and vegetables), a regular fast (one 24-hour period weekly or monthly without food), or a Biblical fast (no food for 1 to 40 days). What other reasons can you think of for you, personally, to fast?

_____

_____

_____

_____

_____

_____

_____

_____

III-7

8. How much fasting do you feel the Lord wants you to do on a regular basis? Have you ever gone on a spiritual fast? What was it like? What did you pray about, or what occupied your time? Did you draw closer to God? How? Have you ever thought of fasting on a regular basis? For what purpose? Do you think there's a right and wrong way to fast? What do you hear the Lord telling you about fasting?

_____

_____

_____

_____

_____

_____

_____

_____

_____

9. What questions do you have about fasting? Do you believe fasting was a custom meant only for those in the Bible? Not only the "spiritual" people fasted in Bible times, it was an ordinary part of life (like feast days) to the average person. What makes you different, living today, from an average Christian who fasted in Bible times? Nothing. The average Christian should also fast. Did you know there are several ways to fast and different reasons to fast? Do you know how to get yourself through a fast healthfully? Do you expect to fight the devil during or after a fast? Are you in submission to God in this area? (Zechariah 7:5)

_____

_____

_____

_____

_____

_____

_____

_____

_____

10. Define the sins of gluttony and slothfulness. Gluttony is the sin of lusting after food and gorging yourself on whatever food delights you at any time, without regard to the physical needs of your body. Slothfulness is another sin affecting the physical side of your nature. This indulgence of the flesh is similar to gluttony. Gluttony has you too active about food; slothfulness has you not active enough about labor.

_____

_____

_____

_____

_____

_____

_____

_____

11. How important is outward appearance to you? You know it's sinful to be vain or overly concerned with the way you look. Growing socially (in favor with men), however, you can't escape the fact people look on the outward appearance. Being a witness for Jesus, an ambassador for Christ, you must be aware of the impression you make with your appearance. The Noble Woman paid attention to her appearance. She wasn't afraid to dress herself in nice, above average clothes.

_____

_____

_____

_____

_____

_____

_____

_____

III-7

12. Do you view yourself as a disciplined person? Do you organize your time? Do you redeem your time with worthwhile activities? Do you know how your time is divided throughout the day? Do you usually accomplish most of what you want throughout the day? Are there always activities, plans, and projects you want to do but never seem to have time for? Are you able to finish projects you start? (Discipline is the force that helps you overcome the sins of gluttony and slothfulness mentioned above. Discipline is the impetus to producing fruit for God's kingdom. The Noble Woman had to be disciplined to accomplish all she did.)

_____

_____

_____

_____

_____

_____

_____

_____

_____

13. Are you in good general health? Having good health is certainly a precious gift. The Noble Woman had good health. She was able to enjoy an active physical life. She had strength and energy. If you aren't in good general health, what things can you do to make yourself healthier?

_____

_____

_____

_____

_____

14. What health problems do you have? What behavior changes are you making to let them heal? A lot of minor health problems today are the result of bad physical habits. Most of these minor problems can be handled by changing your lifestyle. You, as a Christian, have the advantage of having the Holy Spirit to assure you that your behavior can change.

_____

_____

_____

_____

_____

_____

_____

_____

_____

15. What are your beliefs on healing? How do these beliefs apply to you, in particular? Christians who believe in healing for themselves have claimed a gift of the Holy Spirit that greatly enhances their life on earth. God takes care of His children. He has provided wise guidelines in the Bible that, when followed, will keep you in good general health. In addition, He has given the Christian an alternative (or the additional help) of doctors and medicine in overcoming sickness. *"Is any one of you sick? He should call the elders of the church to pray over him and anoint him with oil in the name of the Lord. And the prayer offered in faith will make the sick person well; the Lord will raise him up "* (James 5:14-15).

_____

_____

_____

_____

_____

_____

_____

_____

_____

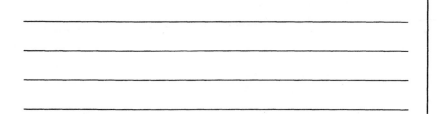

III-7

SUMMARY

In today's culture you must guard against the extremes of body worship. The image of womanhood displayed in television commercials and on billboards is not necessarily the goal God has for you. However, Paul says bodily exercise has some value (I Timothy 4:8). As a Christian, you should be more interested in spiritual goals than physical ones, but that doesn't excuse you from paying attention to the body's needs of nutritious food, exercise, and sleep.

ASSIGNMENT

Memorize Proverbs 3:4-6. Don't forget to review Romans 6. Realize how much you've grown in wisdom through the memorization of these verses.

Suggestion: Put it to music. Have you ever caught yourself singing a commercial jingle? Millions of dollars are spent on commercials that have catchy tunes just to help you remember the product's name. Music does amazing things to words. People who can't memorize a phone number have no trouble remembering scores of lyrics to popular songs. King David, who wrote the Psalms, knew that music helps memory. He set his words to music. Try singing the verses you're trying to memorize. Find a familiar or simple tune that will rise and fall with the pattern of the verses, and discover how quickly memorization takes place.

Lesson 8
Rebuilding the Temple

III-8

PURPOSE

To submit your body to God for Him to rebuild the way He wants it.

OVERVIEW

At every social gathering including women, the topic of conversation will at least once revolve around dieting. It's no secret today's women feel a great responsibility to be slim. Women through the ages have worked for their time's ideal of beauty. It would be incorrect to say God isn't interested in beauty. While it's true God's main concern is with inward beauty (Proverbs 31:30), He doesn't believe in neglecting the body. God intends for bodies to be healthy and strong, not lazy and fat.

God provided a plan in His Word for combating the sin of gluttony and keeping your body fit. Maintained health and vigor should be your goal in adult life. Begin to see your body from God's perspective. It can be programmed and disciplined to perform at peak efficiency. You can build your body into a fortress against disease. You can run your body on better, longer-lasting energy. You can have strength for new and greater tasks. Your body can be a healthy temple as a witness for Jesus Christ. It will enable you to fulfill your purpose in life more efficiently and with more results. In order to rebuild your body God's way, look closely at what God's Word has to say about diet and exercise.

DISCUSSION

When the physical aspect is out of balance, it can greatly influence your growth in the remaining three areas. Physical problems can affect your mind and your perception of wisdom. Poor health, excess weight, and lack of energy certainly retard social development and relationships with family members. And, of course, disobedience in this area causes difficulty in spiritual growth. There are four physical requirements referred to in the Bible. Although man doesn't live by bread alone, he certainly needs to eat to stay alive. God discusses food in the Bible. He told His children what they should and shouldn't eat. Fasting is the second requirement. Though many physicians argue the value of fasting, the truth is, God's Word endorses it for Christians, especially now that we're awaiting Christ's return (Matthew 9:15). Sleep and exercise are the body's two other requirements. They, too, are discussed in the Bible. What does the Bible say about each of these four physical requirements?

Food:

Your lifestyle should be a combination of hard work and eating off the "fat of the land." Food is merely fuel for the body's furnace. It produces energy for labor. Food can be divided into two categories — food you should eat, and food you shouldn't eat. Food is given by God (Psalm 136:25). God has much to say when it comes to what and how you should eat. There are general attitudes about food God wants you to have as guidelines to your eating habits.

1. Matthew 6:31. Don't worry about what you'll eat. Jesus used this specific need when discussing worry with his disciples. Jesus insisted that if you seek God first He will always take care of your physical needs, including providing food for you to eat. Don't worry in social situations about what you have to eat (if nothing is on your diet, for example). God is in charge of the food provided.

2. Proverbs 16:26; I Samuel 30:12; Acts 9:19. Food's purpose is to revive your spirit and give you strength, not to provide comfort or love.

3. I Samuel 9:13. Eat with thankfulness to God; recognize His provision as you eat. This explains the custom of praying before meals. It isn't enough to eat the right food for your health; be **thankful** for it.

4. Proverbs 15:17 and 17:1. Don't eat when you don't have peace in your home. Stress and strife affect digestion.

5. Matthew 6:11. Ask God to daily provide your food. Food was at the top of Jesus' list of requests in His example of prayer.

6. Proverbs 20:1; Ephesians 5:18. Avoid beer and wine. It takes the smallest amount of alcohol to make one legally drunk. This liquid drug adds wasted calories and is a poor substitute for food.

7. Romans 14:2, 14, and 23. Eat according to your convictions. Some people have certain restrictions when it comes to food. They believe they shouldn't eat certain foods, or kinds of food, for reasons of health or weight. If they go against their convictions, they'll certainly suffer for it.

8. I Timothy 4:2-5. Although it's true God put several limitations on the diet of the Israelites, the New Testament clearly states that God has approved all food. God's rules were designed to keep the Israelites healthy. They were to abstain from food such as pork because of the lack of sanitation and refrigeration (Deuteronomy 14:4-21); they couldn't eat animals they found dead because of the possibility of disease (Exodus 22:31). Foods that were eaten in Bible times, however, give a good idea of the kinds of food God intended man to rely on for the bulk of his energy needs. The four food groups are equally represented. Meals of fruit and bread, vegetables and bread, or protein and bread were common. There was a variety of protein available—almonds, beans, beef, cheese, eggs, fish, fowl, locusts, nuts, venison.

Food Abuses:

The Bible discusses gluttony and slothfulness. Gluttony isn't confined to the overweight. It also affects those people who are slim but have trouble controlling their appetites. Gluttony allows your appetite and tastes to rule what, when, and how much you eat, and takes over your life. Additional food disorders, anorexia and bulimia, as well as gluttony, put the concern about food way out of proportion to your needs. An obsession with food can lead to undernourishment for the sake of attaining an unhealthy, underweight body.

III-8

You must be healthy to have energy to serve God and His people. Certain eating habits are good for you; others are detrimental. If you can't identify bad eating habits in your life, you probably need to do more reading about nutrition. Nutrition has become an area of interest to most Americans; but it can also become another obsession. Strive to maintain simple health habits about when you eat, how much you eat, what kind of food you eat, and how you eat. Becoming a Noble Woman involves balance. Don't indulge in habits of eating too much food or food that's too rich. A Noble Woman fills her mouth with praise for God (Psalm 71:8). However, don't stop eating everything you enjoy or greatly reduce your daily intake of calories.

Slothfulness often leads to eating disorders. It's a strong lack of motivation and extreme laziness that keeps you in "low gear" throughout your day. It keeps you in bed too long; on the phone too long; watching television too long; and relaxing too long, and too often. This sin destroys productivity. You don't fulfill your purpose in life; you accomplish little for God, your family, others, or yourself. Not having a clear direction or purpose in life can lead to this sin. A Noble Woman should safeguard herself against slothfulness. She should have a clear purpose in life. Have direction and a goal for healthy food habits. Don't be lazy or unwilling to give up old pleasures for the sake of keeping God's temple pure.

There are many books and reports on the market today about nutrition. It's possible to read an entire book about just one of your body's vitamin requirements. God's method of nutrition is much simpler and more helpful to your body, and especially to your hectic lifestyle.

Fasting:

Built into God's kingdom is a law that would keep you from over-stoking the body's furnace or clogging it with sluggish fuel. The law of the Sabbath was God's way for man and the earth to rest from labor one day out of seven. Interrupting a day-to-day routine of labor with one day of abstinence from normal activity brings needed respite. Experiencing a day of no work revitalizes and motivates you to set yourself to the daily task once again. This law of the Sabbath rest can be applied to your body as well. When you fast, your body takes a needed rest from the daily exertion of digesting food for fuel. Of course, the body still needs energy to operate, but during a fast it has a chance to rest the digestive system and use the extra fuel stored as fat. This process doesn't take place unless digestive juices stop flowing. This is done by drinking only water, and eating no food at all. The only suffering a healthy body experiences during a one day fast is the humble suffering of bringing the flesh into submission to the Spirit.

Besides this physical benefit, why should Christians fast? The Bible has several examples of fasting for reasons of deliverance, revelation, to give power to prayer, to commit someone to God, and to discipline the flesh and suffer for Jesus. The Jewish nation fasted under the leadership of Queen Esther for deliverance from death. David prayed and fasted continually as seen in the Psalms for deliverance from his enemies. Daniel fasted and received revelation from God. The disciples fasted, after Jesus left them, to gain power for their prayers and to commit someone to God (as in Acts 14:23). We commend ourselves as suffering for Jesus by fasting (II Corinthians 6:5).

Jesus went on a 40 day fast. He's our example; but keep in mind He was at the peak of physical and mental health. Diabetics and pregnant women shouldn't fast. Anyone who's doubtful of having optimum health should ask a medical physican for a checkup and advice. Consult a physican who's sympathetic to Christian fasting. The main purpose of a fast is to bring you closer to God. Weight control is a secondary benefit, not a primary target for fasting. The fast itself isn't necessarily intended to cause you to lose weight (most of what you lose will be gained back once you eat again). It's learning self-control, discipline, and submitting to God during a fast that will change your eating patterns for the better. There are many good Christian books about fasting available for those who want to study what the Scriptures say about this exercise of spirit over flesh. Keep in mind Jesus expected Christians to fast (Matthew 9:15).

Sleep:

The first and last word about sleep is found in Psalm 127:2. "*In vain you rise early and stay up late, toiling for food to eat, for he grants sleep to those he loves.*" Just as you learned not to worry about your eating habits, God wants you to learn to trust Him for your sleep as well. God promises His children peaceful sleep (Psalm 4:8) and sweet sleep (Proverbs 3:24). Relax and realize sleep is one of the blessed gifts you receive freely as a Christian. The Bible mentions two conditions that can rob a Christian of sleep — worry and a lack of hard work (Ecclesiates 5:12). Worry and slothfulness are sins. They can affect all areas of growth for a Noble Woman. These sins keep you from getting the kind of sweet, peaceful sleep God intends you to have.

Laziness and the soft life can also produce the opposite — too much sleep. Sleeping too much is linked with poverty in Proverbs 6:9-11, 20:13, and 26:14. **When** you sleep is also important. God says to rise early (Genesis 19:2, Isaiah 16:9). Any sleeping difficulty you might experience can stunt your ability to grow in stature. To overcome sleep irregularities, be sure to do some kind of physical labor throughout the day, go to bed early enough to awaken early; lay your cares on Jesus in prayer; stop worrying; quote Scripture before falling asleep. Waking up during the night can be an opportunity to spend a few minutes in prayer or reviewing memorized Scripture.

When you miss an entire night's sleep or your regular number of hours sleep, your body can't "catch up" the next night. It takes several nights to reset your internal clock to its original pattern. Sometimes it takes external signals to cue your body that you're ready to sleep. If you've conditioned your body with these external signals you might "fool" it into thinking it's sleeping according to its normal pattern if you occasionally have a late night. You can also use these signals to your advantage if you must sleep somewhere other than your own bed. These signals can be as simple as drinking warm milk, reading, and putting your body into a particular position, or as complex as a washing routine, saying prayers, or closing up the house. You should also have cues for waking up. The same alarm or radio station, a cup of coffee in the same cup, or the same bathroom ritual can get you started in the morning even if you've missed some sleep. It doesn't matter what the routine is, as long as you follow some system for healthy sleep habits.

Although physicians think eight hours of sleep is average, some people need less (6 or 7); others need more (8 or 9). Sometimes the way you feel in the morning isn't a good indication of whether or not you had enough sleep. People who reach maximum potential in the afternoon or "night owl" producers are groggy no matter what time they awaken.

Exercise:

Aerobic exercises are very popular now. With the number of injuries rising each year, health enthusiasts are realizing low impact aerobics are better. Doctors across the country agree with the simple exercise God showed us in the Bible. What could be more natural, easy, and healthy than walking? Except for training for battle, there was no need for exercise in Bible times. Daily walking and hard work provided ample opportunity to work the muscles and "rev" up the metabolism.

Other than Paul's reference to exercise in I Timothy 4:7-10, nothing is mentioned in the Bible about exercise for it's own sake. Walking is mentioned often for travel and as a means of fellowship. Adam and Enoch walked with God. In Psalm 55:14, David mentions walking with a friend. Proverb 13:20 describes the advantage of walking with a friend who's wise. The Bible doesn't give any evidence of exercise for personal benefits, but rather partaking a physical activity with a friend for the purpose of fellowship. Instead of relying on your own source of strength from exercise, God wants you to be weak so He can be strong. Isaiah 40:29-31 says He can enable you to run and not get tired and to walk without feeling weak.

Humans are made with four major muscle groups—two in the legs and two in the arms. Each day these muscles need to be worked to some degree. Each muscle group needs to be regularly pushed to a high percentage of its physical limits. This is usually drastically higher than muscles are worked through the course of a normal day.

III-8

However, the law of diminishing return applies to exercise. Once your body gets used to a new workload (such as daily exercise), it adjusts its metabolism to stop losing any more fat or gaining any more muscle. Then, the same amount of exercise must be maintained to keep the body at its new status. A heavier workload must be undertaken to lose fat or gain muscle again. This can become a trap. People shouldn't put unrealistic expectations on their bodies to overperform physically.

SUMMARY

God is concerned about the physical side of your nature. He was careful to include words of instruction in the Bible about what to eat, when to fast, how to sleep, and the value of exercise. When you begin to submit yourself to God in these areas, you're rebuilding your temple of the Holy Spirit. While being careful not to overemphasize the needs of the body, you can have a Godly attitude toward diet and exercise. You must ask the Lord for your daily bread and trust Him to decide what you'll eat. You should look for opportunities to exercise with friends and engage in physical labor. Prayerfully consider fasting on a regular basis; sleep without worry; trust God to take care of your life.

ASSIGNMENT

Memorize Proverbs 3:7-10. You'll learn that fearing and trusting God will bring physical health. The more you memorize the more you grow in wisdom. If you follow the advice in these verses, you'll also begin to grow in stature.

Suggestion: Sleep on it. Did you know the memory mechanisms in the brain are sharper as you sleep? Quote your memory verses as your drop off to sleep and review them first thing when you awaken. You'll be amazed how much you have memorized during sleep.

TABLE 4

GUIDELINES FOR FASTING

1. Abstain from caffeine 2-3 days prior to the fast to avoid caffeine headaches.
2. Drink only warm water so your digestive juices stop flowing.
3. If lightheadedness or cramps seem unbearable, try drinking warm water. Waiting 10-20 minutes before deciding to break the fast. Usually such conditions pass in a few minutes.
4. Come off the fast slowly with small amounts of soups and juices.
5. The longer you fast (up to the point of returned hunger) the easier it will get, and the more spiritual benefits you will achieve.
6. Don't make any major decisions until after you fast.
7. During your fast keep a journal of prayers, insights from the Lord, and what's happening to your mental, physical, and social sides as your spiritual side excels.
8. Decide before you begin when you want to break the fast so the devil cannot tempt you to stop early.

Lesson 9
Growing in Stature

III-9

PURPOSE
To learn how to follow Jesus' example of maintaining health and vigor.

OVERVIEW
Stature may appear to be the easiest area in which to grow but it's difficult to bring the flesh into submission to God. The finer aspects of discipline (selflessness, displaying a merry heart, belief in healing, and keeping busy) are needed to truly deny the flesh and grow in stature.

DISCUSSION
Discipline:
Be diligent (steady, earnest, and energetic) in disciplining (training that corrects, molds, or perfects) yourself. This involves constantly guarding the physical (flesh). Hebrews 12 is an excellent chapter on discipline. God want Christians to endure physical hardship (verse 7) as discipline. Although discipline itself seems hard to endure at the time, benefits do appear when you don't give up (verse 11). You know by now how much discipline is involved in diet, fasting, sleep, and exercise. Be careful to note the distinction between willpower (which is fleshly and sinful) and the power of the Holy Spirit (Zechariah 4:6). It's the Holy Spirit who gives true self-control (Galatians 5:22).

Controlling the appetites of the flesh (too much food, too much sleep, too much or too little exercise, too much pleasure), refer to a lifelong discipline that helps you overcome sins against your body and grow in stature.

Selflessness:
Jesus warned against being out of balance by placing too much emphasis on the physical. II Timothy 3:1-5 says *"But mark this: There will be terrible times in the last days. People will be lovers of themselves, lovers of money, boastful, proud, abusive, disobedient to their parents, ungrateful, unholy, without love, unforgiving, slanderous, without self-control, brutal, not lovers of the good, treacherous, rash, conceited, lovers of pleasure rather than lovers of God — having a form of godliness but denying its power. Have nothing to do with them."* These are strong words for the world today. Christians need to do what God tells them (James 1:22). The Noble Woman was careful to spend much of her time in the selfless pursuit of helping others and taking care of the needs of those less fortunate.

Over 750 verses in the Bible refer to giving to others. A person who pays too much attention to how she looks or how her body feels (or if she's made her daily quota of diet and exercise) seldom has time for the needs of others. A Noble Woman will follow God's Word (Matthew 16:24-27) in picking up the cross of selflessness and denying herself.

Merry Heart:

God didn't ignore happiness and joy when He asked you to deny yourself. In fact, much is said in the Bible about the benefits of a sense of humor or merry heart. Physically, it makes your face pleasant to look at (Proverbs 15:13). A positive outlook can make you see how abundantly your needs are being provided (Proverbs 15:15). Joy helps you grow in stature because it gives you strength (Nehemiah 8:10). If you experience a difficult, weary, or stressful day, cultivate joy by singing joyous songs. If you have a happy day, you should already be singing songs of joy (James 5:13). The laughter and happiness you experience through singing will revive your spirit and give you renewed energy to tackle your tasks. Singing songs of praise is the Christian's equivalent to a coffee break.

If just feeling great isn't enough incentive for you to have a merry heart, read Proverbs 17:22; you'll learn that laughter and joy actually affect the body like good medicine. God wants you to have joy and express it freely. *"Until now you have not asked for anything in my name. Ask and you will receive and your joy will be complete"* (John 16:24).

Healing:

Some Christians get nervous whenever healing is mentioned today. What God intended to be a blessing has brought fear to many. Some fear they'll be criticized for not throwing out medications. Others fear God may not be pleased with them for getting medical attention. The fact that God promises to heal all your diseases cannot be denied (Psalm 103:3), but He does not punish you for lack of faith in this area.

Most of the verses on healing refer to keeping the body in good health. God gives excellent preventative medicine to bring healing to your bones, keeping them healthy and strong; healing to your wounds, for quick recovery; and healing to your whole body. What can you do to attain this healing for your body? In Proverbs 4:22 we're told to keep God's words in our hearts to be healthy. Other healing activities include speaking wisely (Proverbs 12:18), fasting for more than a day (Isaiah 58:8), and speaking or hearing pleasant words (Proverbs 16:24). John's wish for you in III John 2 is that you may enjoy good health.

Labor:

Hard work is one of God's ways to keep the body toned and healthy. We are laborers together with God, according to I Corinthians 3:9. By working hard, you can be confident God will reward you for your labor (I Corinthians 3:8). *"All hard work brings a profit"* (Proverbs 14:23). Besides the physical benefits, labor brings blessings and prosperity (Psalm 128:2). On the other hand, being lazy brings decay and destruction to your life (Ecclesiastes 10:18). I Corinthians has much to say about labor, as in I Corinthians 15:58, *"Always give yourselves fully to the work of the Lord because you know your labor is not in vain."*

III-9

SUMMARY

Growing in stature is more complex than paying attention to diet and exercise. It involves disciplining yourself to do hard work for others with a selfless attitude while maintaining a merry heart. It means believing in health and healing for your body according to God's Word. It entails singing songs of praise and depending on the Holy Spirit for strength. If all this seems more than a Noble Woman can handle, remember Jesus' words in Matthew 11:28-30: *"Come to me, all you who are weary and burdened, and I will give you rest. Take my yoke upon you and learn from me, for I am gentle and humble in heart, and you will find rest for your souls. For my yoke is easy and my burden is light."*

ASSIGNMENT

Memorize Proverbs 3:11-14. God wants to use discipline in your life as a sign of His love for you.

Suggestion: Personalize Scripture. You will remember it longer because it means more to you. For instance, verse 11 could read this way when you personalize it: *"I will not despise the Lord's discipline and I do not resent His rebuke, because the Lord loves me."*

TABLE 5
GOOD HEALTH HABITS FROM THE BIBLE

1. Rise early. Genesis 19:2

2. Work hard. Proverbs 14:23

3. Have a merry heart. Proverbs 17:22

4. Don't eat the rich man's food. Proverbs 23:1

5. Drink plenty of water daily. Exodus 23:25

6. Fast on a regular basis. Isaiah 58:8

7. Run and don't be weary, walk and don't faint. Isaiah 40:29-31

8. Eat a variety of foods. I Timothy 4:2-5

Lesson 10
Self-Evaluation D

PURPOSE

To determine how close you are to Jesus, how much you have grown spiritually since becoming a Christian, and ways in which you can continue to grow in favor with God.

OVERVIEW

In this evaluation you'll answer personal questions about the time you spend with God. Sometimes people think they're spending adequate time praying and reading the Bible until they have to name the actual number of minutes spent in prayer, who they prayed for, or the Bible chapters they read. This evauation then, is to help you accurately record time spent with God and in Godly activities on a daily basis. Answer as honestly as you can. It's better to underestimate yourself in this area than overestimate.

SELF-EVALUATION

1. What's your daily plan for Bible study and time alone with God? Have you found time in your busy day to be alone with God? Do you give Him the first part of each day by praising Him as you arise? Do you have a pattern or routine you follow in your quiet time with God? How do you study your Bible? How many Bible versions do you have? Explain why you have each version.

_____

_____

_____

_____

_____

_____

_____

_____

_____

_____

2. Do you have a plan for deeper Bible study? What Bible
reference books and Christian inspirational books do you own?
What non-fiction Christian books have you read that have
influenced your walk with the Lord? Do you regularly read both
Christian inspirational books and non-fiction Christian books?

_____

_____

_____

_____

_____

_____

_____

_____

3. What deeper study do you think God wants you to make? Are
there Bible subjects or characters you would like to learn more
about? Are there topics that you don't understand concerning
Christians? Do you wonder if the Bible really says what you think
it does about certain issues?

_____

_____

_____

_____

_____

_____

_____

_____

4. Do you have a plan for Bible memorization? What makes you
decide to memorize a Bible verse? Do you memorize every day?
Every week? Do you review verses you've already memorized?

Explain your plan for Bible memorization.

_____

_____

_____

_____

_____

_____

_____

_____

IV-10

5. What subjects or chapters do you think God wants you to memorize? Has God touched your life with a verse or chapter in the Bible? Do certain kinds of verses bless you more than others? Are there chapters in the Bible that stand out in your mind as helpful, encouraging, comforting, or promising? God makes certain Bible verses stand out when you read them so you'll feel a burden to meditate further and, possibly, memorize them. The workings of God's kingdom are varied and vast; the gifts of the Holy Spirit are different; a different gift is bestowed upon each person. Because of this, He may give everyone different verses to memorize.

_____

_____

_____

_____

_____

_____

_____

_____

_____

6. How do you memorize and review Scripture? Be specific. How many days does it take you to learn one verse by heart? What method do you use to review? How do you keep track of verses you've memorized, those you're now memorizing, and those you'd like to memorize?

_____

_____

_____

_____

_____

_____

_____

_____

_____

7. Name non-Christians you're interested in helping bring to salvation (by prayer, witnessing, bringing to church, etc.). There are many ways to be a witness for Jesus and lead others to Him. Everyone you meet is somewhere along the road toward Jesus. Your example of what a Christian is truly like can influence their chances of reaching the end of that road and beginning a relationship with Jesus; but those you meet aren't the only people you can influence. Do you pray for anyone, anywhere in the world, whether you know them well or not? New Christians may be born out of fellow workers, relatives, past or present friends. God doesn't want you to assume a "witnessing personality," but rather be yourself. Is your conversation filled with natural references to your faith, your church life, and your relationship with God? If you notice your conversation seldom touches on the subject of Jesus, perhaps your own relationship with Him needs to be strengthened so you can let your "light so shine before men."

_____

_____

_____

_____

_____

_____

_____

_____

_____

8. In addition to being a witness to the lost, a Christian has a responsibility to his brothers and sisters in Christ. The apostle Paul says to encourage each other in the faith. Someone who has

become born again (John 3) doesn't automatically become knowledgeable about Jesus and the things of God. *"We know that we have passed from death to life, because we love our brothers"* (I John 3:14). Discipleship means following the example of Jesus by teaching Christians who are drawn to your personality and are hungry to know more about God. Do you spend time on an individual or group basis in fellowship and prayer with new Christians? Do you tell them what you know about Jesus and the Bible? Name Christians you are interested in bringing closer to Jesus or discipling in small or large ways.

IV-10

_____

_____

_____

_____

_____

_____

_____

_____

_____

9. Are you being discipled personally by a strong Christian woman? Although it isn't recorded, we can surmise by studying Jewish customs that the Noble Woman was taught the things she knew about being a wife, mother, and servant to God and man. When it comes to being a Noble Woman, experiences' partner is personal discipleship. If you've had trouble growing spiritually, maybe you've lacked leadership and direction. Older women are to teach younger women how to be the best they can be (Titus 2:4). The movement away from the extended family has broken down God's planned method of discipleship. It's up to you now, to find an older Christian woman to disciple you. Be sure she's closer to the Lord than you are and in a position with God and the Church that you would like to be in yourself. Her relationship with God should be evidenced by her conversation, church activities, church support, dependence on God, prayer life, praise of God, concern for others, and Bible knowledge. Pray and ask God to lead you to such a woman. List possible disciplers and approach them about your need for someone to help you grow as a Christian. Ask them to pray about discipling you. Trust God to bring the right woman into your life.

_____

_____

_____

_____

_____

_____

_____

_____

_____

10. Do you have a regular prayer life? Prayer is the essence of a Christian's relationship to God. If you don't talk to God, how can you say you have a relationship with Him? Do you consider yourself distantly or closely related to God? Are you able to confide everything to Jesus? Even occasional bad feelings towards Him? Do you consider yourself a prayer warrior? Are you a strong or weak pray-er? How often do you pray? For how long? How do you pray when someone asks you to pray for him? Do you often pray for others? Do you pray at the same time each day? In the same place? Since you've been a Christian, how has your prayer life changed and grown?

_____

_____

_____

_____

_____

_____

_____

_____

11. Have you set time aside or do you occasionally feel God calling you to times of deeper prayer? Have you ever prayed for an hour? Several hours? Have you ever attended a prayer meeting and spent several hours praying there? Have you ever been awakened by the Holy Spirit during the night with a prayer concern? Have you ever prayed through the night? Why? Have you ever prayed for the same person or prayer need several days in a row? Have you ever felt extremely burdened about a prayer need? Do you have questions about prayer? What do you know the Bible says about prayer? What kind of prayer life do you think you should have?

_____

_____

_____

_____

_____

_____

_____

_____

IV-10

12. Name different people, things, and situations you regularly pray for. What motivates you to pray for something or someone? Do you believe God gives you what you ask for? Do you believe God wants you to pray for others? For countries? For leaders of countries? Do you pray for your President? Your mayor? Your pastor and elders? Do you have a prayer partner? Are you on a church prayer chain? Do you attend a regular church prayer meeting? **What** you pray for is just as important as **when** and **how** you pray. Do you understand the different kinds of prayer? Do you know what prayer is? How it works? Do you think God can hear you when you pray? Do you listen to God when you pray? How are most of your prayers answered? Is prayer hard work for you?

_____

_____

_____

_____

_____

_____

_____

_____

13. Christians pray with many varied styles. Some prefer to meet God through praise and speak to Him as if in natural conversation with a friend. Others are more detailed, following lists of people, countries, and needs with a different list each day of the week. Some write out their prayers, recording the anguish, joy, suffering, peace, and submission they deal with concerning their prayers. A prayer list can be a list of names, subjects to pray about, or prayer requests and needs. A prayer list can be a mental rundown of prayer for the lost first, followed by leaders,

friends, family, and finally, yourself. Or it can be a written list that changes daily, monthly, or when the need arises. Often people list personal prayer requests and the date God answers them. No matter what method you use, it's good to have a system for praying. The need for prayer is great; the list of who and what you should pray for is too long to be committed solely to memory. Do you have a prayer list? Describe it briefly.

_____

_____

_____

_____

_____

_____

_____

_____

14. Do you know what your spiritual gifts are? Every Christian has received gifts from God. Salvation is a gift. The ability to love others is a gift. God has given you a gift to help you serve your church family (Acts 2:38). No Christian is permitted to grow and live separate from the Body of Christ. No Christian should allow himself to only receive from others in the Church without giving back to them in some way. God is no respecter of persons. He gives equally to all who ask. When you became a Christian, the Holy Spirit gave you a special gift, a talent to give to the Church (Romans 12:6, I Corinthians 7:7). The gifts you have aren't just to be enjoyed by yourself or your immediate family, but by the entire family of God. Do you know which of your talents could be used in the Church? Are you trying to be involved in at least one ministry in your church? In what ways have you used your spiritual gifts for other Christians?

_____

_____

_____

_____

_____

_____

_____

IV-10

15. Do you need to know more about your gifts and how to use them? *"Now about the spiritual gifts, brothers, I do not want you to be ignorant"* (I Corinthians 12:1). The Noble Woman needs to understand her spiritual gifts. *"Eagerly desire spiritual gifts"* (I Corinthians 14:1). Study I Corinthians if you lack knowledge about the spiritual gifts. Remember when searching for your gifts, they won't be exactly the same as someone else's (I Corinthians 12:4). If you know what your gifts are but haven't been using them fully for the Lord, follow the advice in II Timothy 4:14, *"Do not neglect your gift,"* and in II Timothy 1:6, *"Fan into flame the gift of God."*

_____

_____

_____

_____

_____

_____

_____

_____

_____

16. Though it's easy to identify the ministries of the Sunday school teacher, choir member, or nursery worker, there are many personal ministries which can be developed inside or outside the church. Are you a good listener? A church prayer chain, counselor, or right-hand assistant to a ministry director might be your gift of service. Do you love to sew? Organize a sewing group or personally sew outfits for missionaries or the poor. Sew uniforms for a Christian school. Do you write long, delightful letters? Become familiar with the hospital visitation list and write letters to members who are hospitalized or homebound. (Even if you don't know them personally, you can identify yourself as a church member; this will keep them feeling loved by and supportive of their church.) Or write letters to visitors of the church, or to church missionaries, who love to hear from fellow Americans. There are endless possibilities for personal ministry. Let your personal ministry dictate how involved you'll be in other church activities. It's better to do a few things well than feel responsible to serve in every area of need in the Church. What do you think is your personal ministry from God? Why?

_____

_____

_____

_____

_____

_____

_____

_____

_____

17. Which fruit of the Holy Spirit do you need developed most in your life? *"The fruit of the Spirit is love, joy, peace, patience, kindness, goodness, faithfulness, gentleness, and self-control"* (Galatians 5:22). Your personality determines which fruit of the Holy Spirit you have particular trouble developing. Do you know which fruit is **least** developed in your life? Have you made efforts to plant seeds of that fruit in the lives of others to help "raise a crop" in your own life?

_____

_____

_____

_____

_____

_____

_____

_____

_____

SUMMARY

God's greatest equalizer for Christians, other than time, is prayer. It's the spiritual activity He has given every Christian as a means to produce fruit for Him. Anyone, anywhere, any age, in any physical condition, rich or poor, can pray. It's not so much the activities in your life that determine favor with God, but time spent in prayer communicating with the One through whom all can be accomplished. Just as Job, the man God called the greatest on earth, was humbled through prayer, so you too will find it difficult to sin while speaking to the Almighty God. Growing in favor with God refers to those private areas of your Christian life. God is more interested in what you **are** than what you **do.**

68

ASSIGNMENT

Memorize Proverbs 3:15-18. As you memorize, appreciate how you are growing in favor with God by hiding His Word in your heart.

Suggestion: As you learn to grow in favor with God, you'll have the opportunity to apply your Bible memorization to prayer. Pray about the verses you're trying to memorize. Ask God to help you remember the words, understand their meaning, and apply the words to your daily life.

IV-10

Lesson 11
Time with God

IV-11

PURPOSE

To discover how to spend time with God.

OVERVIEW

Spending time with God can be easy and natural (or as stilted and artificial) as speaking with those persons closest to you. If you've developed a loving, intimate, honest, and encouraging relationship with anyone else, it shouldn't be difficult to have the same kind of relationship with God. Your relationship to God can be compared to the best of several kinds of relationships on earth. This lesson examines possible relationships with God. The kind of relationship you have with God determines how you spend time with Him. Whether you refer to this time as quiet time, devotions, or prayer time, it's important to set time aside and meet with God on a regular basis.

DISCUSSION

Jesus is the example to follow for spending time with God. He often went into the hills to be alone with God (Matthew 14:23, Luke 9:18 and 28). If He, Who is perfect, needed to spend time with His Father, how much more do others? You should repeat the words of David (a man after God's own heart) in Psalm 5:3 *"Morning by morning, O Lord, you hear my voice; morning by morning I lay my requests before you and wait in expectation."*

Now that the importance of meeting with God has been established, you can identify the kinds of relationships you can have with Him. This lesson begins with the most formal and ends with the most intimate.

King/subject:

"For God is the King of all the earth" (Psalm 47:7). In I Samuel, when the nation of Israel asked God for a king, He was disappointed in them. He wanted to be their only king; He didn't want them to look toward men for leadership. Today He wants to be king of your heart and Lord of every area of your life. Fearing God is a way to obtain wisdom. "Fearing" God merely means honoring Him as King. In your time with Him, you should acknowledge this relationship and reverence His almighty majesty. One day every nation will proclaim Him Lord of lords and King of kings (Isaiah 45:23, Romans 14:11, Philippians 2:10).

Shepherd/sheep:

"We all, like sheep, have gone astray" (Isaiah 53:6). The Bible identifies Christians as sheep, as does Jesus, in the sense that both can easily get lost. You can forsake wisdom and follow a

crowd headed for destruction. Both are loved and protected by the Good Shepherd (John 10:14). Psalm 23 best describes this relationship:

Vs. 1: *"The Lord is my shepherd, I shall lack nothing."* As a shepherd provides for his sheep, God provides for all your needs.

Vs. 2: *"He makes me lie down in green pastures, he leads me beside quiet waters."* Sometimes God has to "make" you move toward His promises. He provides your physical needs.

Vs. 3: *"He restores my soul. He guides me in paths of righteousness for his name's sake."* God provides for your spiritual need to have peace with Him, and to know right from wrong.

Vs. 4: *"Even though I walk through the valley of the shadow of death, I will fear no evil, for you are with me; your rod and your staff, they comfort me."* God provides for your mental needs by supplying emotional comfort.

Vs. 5: *"You prepare a table before me in the presence of my enemies. You anoint my head with oil; my cup overflows."* God provides your social needs by giving you honor and social acceptance among those who have mistreated you.

Vs. 6: *"Surely goodness and love will follow me all the days of my life."* God provides your needs on this earth, during your lifetime.

Vs. 7: *"...and I will dwell in the house of the Lord forever."* God will also provide your needs in heaven.

Like sheep, Christians are defenseless and weak, easily led astray by the evil one. The Good Shepherd gently nudges them in the right direction. He wants you to ask Him for your daily needs and direction. By petitioning Him during your devotional time you relate to God as your Shepherd.

Father/child:

When you receive correction or conviction from God, you call Him Father (Proverbs 3:12). You confess your sins to the Father. In fact, all prayer is part of the Father/child relationship. This is a more intimate relationship than the previous two because there's a more personal exchange. You honor God as **king,** from a distance, because all of mankind is subject to Him. You're a **sheep** to the good shepherd even while you're lost and don't react to His provision. Being a **child** is a matter of choice. Jesus opens the door for you to become an actual son of God, so you can relate to Him as a child; because of Jesus you become a child (John 14:6). As the story of the prodigal son reveals, God rejoices when you become a son. As a sheep you couldn't recognize your dependence on God; as a son you can truly love Him. Now, in addition to asking God for your daily needs, you can ask for your desires as well (John 14:14). You can ask your Father for anything. While the mediator between God and you **is** Jesus (John 14:13-14), Jesus said to pray to your father. Matthew 6 contains Jesus' advice on how to pray and develop your Father/ child relationship:

Vs. 6: *"When you pray, go into your room, close the door and pray* *to your father, who is unseen.*" You're to have a private relationship with God.

Vs. 7: "*And when you pray, do not keep on babbling like pagans, for they think they will be heard because of their many words.*" God wants you to pray specifically for what you need or want and not be repetitious. God hears when you pray. He listens as a loving Father.

Vs. 9: "*Our Father in heaven…*" God resides in heaven. One day you will live there with Him as an intimate family member.

Vs. 10: "*Your kingdom come, your will be done on earth as it is in heaven.*" God wants you to obey Him on earth.

Vs. 11: "*Give us today our daily bread.*" He wants you to ask Him daily for what you need.

Vs. 12: "*Forgive us our debts, as we also have forgiven our debtors.*" He wants you to forgive.

Vs. 13: "*And lead us not into temptation, but deliver us from the evil one.*" God wants to protect you from evil.

IV-11

You'll study more about prayer in the next two lessons. Through your prayer life you develop your relationship as God's child.

Master/disciple:

As you develop a more intimate relationship with God, you call Him "Master." In John 13:13 Jesus said you're right to call Him "Teacher." The disciples spoke of Jesus as the "Master" or "Teacher" because He taught them how to live righteously. Jesus expounded on Scripture in a way that helped His disciples understand how to live God's will. They followed Jesus and His advice. They were willing to learn. He's your "Master" in the same way when you read the New Testament and apply it to your Christian walk. He helps you grow in wisdom, stature, and favor. He can show you things about your personal needs, your family, and your friends. This is the intimate relationship of Master/disciple, more intimate than the other relationships because of the greater exchange going on between you and God. You honor the King from a distance; you receive provision from the Shepherd; you enjoy love and discipline from the Father; but you learn how to be a Christian (and a Noble Woman) on a daily basis from the Master.

God knows He's your Master when He sees you apply what you've learned and do what He says. Pay close attention when you read God's Word and you'll develop a Master/disciple relationship with Him.

Brother/sibling:

As you become closer to God by spending time with Him, you may feel the special bond that is present between brothers. Jesus didn't want to distance Himself from man. He was every bit a man (except for the sin nature), and at the same time every bit of God. Because God came down to earth in the form of a man, He can be your brother. He made a point of saying, in Matthew 12:50, that when you do God's will, you are His brother.

This relationship, being God's brother, has been explained throughout the Bible as one of mutual love and concern for each other's interests and burdens. Being God's brother, you gain certain privileges. Jesus' inheritance is yours also. You'll rule and reign with Him (Revelation 5:10). In this relationship with God, you share burdens. You accept God's burden for the lost and perishing of this world as your own (II Peter 3:9). When you pray for others, you relate to Jesus as your brother.

Friend/friend:

As you move into the relationship of Friend/friend, you'll see this beautiful intimacy expressed in John 15:

Vs. 9: *"As the Father has loved me, so have I loved you. Now remain in my love."* Being a friend of God is a matter of choice. You don't choose your family members; but you do choose your friends. People become friends by the amount of time they spend together, the respect and admiration they have for each other, and the interests and concerns they share.

Vs. 10: *"If you obey my commands, you will remain in my love, just as I have obeyed my Father's commands and remain in his love."* Friendships are maintained by constantly remaining in touch. In order to keep God as your friend you must remain in constant contact.

Vs. 11: *"I have told you this so that my joy may be in you and that your joy may be complete."* Friends enjoy each other's company. God wants you to enjoy spending time with Him.

Vs. 12-13: *"My command is this: Love each other as I have loved you. Greater love has no one than this, that one lay down his life for his friends."* God gave the ultimate gesture of friendship by dying on the cross for you. You, in turn, are to pick up His cross and deny yourself for Him.

Vs. 14-15: *"You are my friends if you do what I command. I no longer call you servants, because a servant does not know his master's business. Instead, I have called you friends, for everything that I learned from my Father I have made known to you."* As you move through the relationships of Master/disciple and Brother/sibling to Friend/friend, you see how God reveals more of His business. He truly is a friend who is closer than a brother (Proverbs 18:24).

Husband/wife:

The most intimate relationship known to man is that of husband and wife. Scriptures say they are one in flesh and spirit. Is it any wonder, then, that God refers to the Christian body of believers as the "Bride of Christ?" In Paul's exposition in Ephesians 5, he gives a clue, in verse 32, that he's not just discussing the relationship of a husband and wife, but the relationship between Christ and the Church:

Vs. 23: *"For the husband is the head of the wife as Christ is the head of the church, his body, of which he is the Savior."* You're to allow God to head your life and make decisions concerning your life.

Vs. 24: *"Now as the church submits to Christ, so also wives should submit to their husbands in everything."* Only when you are this intimate with God do you submit to Him in everything.

Vs. 25: *"Husbands, love your wives, just as Christ loved the church and gave himself up for her."* God loves you by giving Himself to you in every way.

Vs. 26: *". . . to make her holy, cleansing her by the washing with water through the word."* When you open up totally to God, He makes you holy on the inside.

Vs. 27: *" . . . and to present her to himself as a radiant church, without stain or wrinkle or any other blemish, but holy and blameless."* You're presented to God as a bride glowing in pure white radiance.

Vs. 28: *"In this same way, husbands ought to love their wives as their own bodies. He who lives his wife loves himself."* God loves you as Himself.

Vs. 29-30: *"After all, no one ever hated his own body, but he feeds and cares for it, just as Christ does the church — for we are members of his body."* He cares for you as a new bride.

Vs. 32: *"This is a profound mystery — but I am talking about Christ and the church."* This mystery is revealed to those most intimate with God.

How wonderful to know that then you spend time with God you can achieve this ultimate intimacy.

IV-11

What to Do When Spending Time with God

1. **Set time aside.** You must decide how many minutes, times a day, and days a week you'll spend alone with God. How long you pray is up to you. The only mention of the length of time spent in prayer is when Jesus asked His disciples, in the garden of Gethsemene, if they could pray for just one hour (Mark 14:37). Jesus spent entire nights in prayer, as well as praying for hours during the early morning. It seems the least you're to offer, then, is one hour. How many times a day? There are many precedents in the Bible. Psalm 88:13 says David prayed morning and evening. He added noontime as well (Psalm 55:17). Daniel prayed three times a day (Daniel 6:13). Psalm 119:164 mentions praising God seven times daily. There's no question that those in the Bible who prayed did so daily.

2. **Read your Bible.** II Timothy 3:16 says the Old Testament (Scripture) is given to help you live righteously. Bible reading can be done in many ways. Many gain wisdom by reading Proverbs daily; there's a chapter for every day of the month. Others find reading Psalms in the morning fills their life with praise and joy. There are many devotionals which help you read through the Bible in a year or study characters or subjects in the Bible. The key is to provide variety in your Bible reading over the years. Don't limit yourself only to the New Testament or only one Bible version. The Holy Spirit will give you new insights and your interest will be renewed with each kind of Bible study you try.

3. **Memorize Scripture.** Learning Bible verses by heart helps you overcome sin, remember what God wants you to do, witness to others, and renew your spiritual growth (Psalm 119:11).

4. **Read Christian study books.** I Thessalonians 5:11 is a basis for adding Bible based non-fiction books to your time with God. Don't let this reading take up more time than your Bible reading. These books are only supplementary. Books by such authors as Watchman Nee, C.S. Lewis, Chuck Swindoll, Anne Ortlund, or Tim and Beverly LaHaye (among others) can inspire, encourage, explain Scripture, organize Bible knowledge, and lead you to recognition of sin, repentance, and action.

5. **Listen to tapes.** These can be Bible tapes or teaching tapes about Bible subjects. Romans 10:17 identifies hearing as a necessary element for faith. Using tapes is especially helpful if you must squeeze time with God into a too hectic schedule. Jogging while listening to the Bible, or driving to work listening to a Bible teacher is an adequate addition to your time with God. Be sure you also have time alone with God without distraction.

6. **Meditate on God's Word.** The devil has taken God's positive method of meditation and abused it greatly in our society. God commanded Christians to meditate on His words only, and to do it day and night (Joshua 1:8). It's not the same as memorizing, although meditation helps you memorize. To meditate you must spend a large amount of time on a few words in the Bible. Take a Bible verse, break it down, and think about what God is telling you personally in every word. Dwell on God's majesty and His love for you. To meditate is to learn the art of praising God for His revelation through Scripture. It's **not** emptying the mind, or reciting meaningless words, or even visualizing something.

7. **Pray.** Over and over. Scripture reminds you to call upon God in prayer (Jeremiah 33:3). You become strong against the enemy when you pray. You work hand-in-hand with God when you pray. You accomplish His will when you pray. Develop the habit of asking God for your daily needs. Don't be afraid to ask him for your desires as well. Always pray for others. Pray for those who are lost spiritually and for those who witness to others.

SUMMARY

As a Christian you should be able to hear God's voice calling you to spend time developing a relationship with Him. How much time you spend on a regular basis determines how close a relationship you have with Him. As a Noble Woman you should know God as your King, Shepherd, Father, Master, Brother, Friend, and Husband. Be careful to set aside time daily to spend with God by praying, reading your Bible, memorizing Scripture, and meditating on that Scripture.

ASSIGNMENT

Memorize Proverbs 3:19-20. You will then have almost doubled your Scripture memorization. Be sure to spend time with God doing the other activities mentioned as well.

Suggestion: Faith comes from actually hearing God's Word. Tape the Scripture you want to memorize or use your Bible tapes to hear God's Word being spoken. Recite the words along with the tape for faster memorization.

IV-11

Lesson 12
Growing in Favor with God

IV-12

PURPOSE

To discover what God expects you to do in ministering to the Body of Christ.

OVERVIEW

After developing your relationship with God, you need to continue to grow in His favor. Do the spiritual work He appointed you. *"All this is from God, who reconciled us to himself through Christ and gave us the ministry of reconciliation"* (II Corinthians 5:18). You have a responsibility to be a witness to non-Christians. You also have a responsibility to minister to the Body of Christ in the local church. To grow in favor with God you must live up to your responsibilities. Strive to please Him by setting aside time to meet the needs of others through the spiritual work He has called you to do. Everyone has to carry his load when it comes to fulfilling God's plan in reaching the non-Christian and serving fellow Christians (Galatians 6:5). Let us agree with the words in I Timothy 1:12, *"I thank Christ Jesus our Lord, who has given me strength, that he considered me faithful, appointing me to his service."*

It is safe to surmise the Noble Woman's spiritual gift was "helps" since she displayed this gift at every opportunity. This lesson will take a closer look at witnessing and using the gifts of the Holy Spirit to minister.

DISCUSSION

Ministry to Non-Christians:

"But you, keep your head in all situations, endure hardship, do the work of an evangelist, discharge all the duties of your ministry" (II Timothy 4:5). Jesus was speaking to every Christian when He said, "You will be my witnesses." In Matthew 5:13-16 He called Christians salt and light. As salt, you should make others thirsty to know Jesus. As light, you are to let Jesus' love and truth shine through you to overcome the darkness of evil in the world, and spark new life in Christ in others. As II Timothy 4:5 denotes, as a witness for Jesus you must be balanced so you can "keep your head" and endure hardship. It's difficult to witness to someone if you take offense at every criticism he has of you, Christianity or the Bible. To truly be an evangelist to unsaved family, co-workers, and service people, you must endure embarrassed looks and being misunderstood or disliked.

Being a witness for Jesus doesn't mean you have to force each non-Christian you meet to pray to accept Jesus as his Savior.

If someone asks how to live this life or how to become a Christian, there are two easy methods you can use to explain the process.

First is the "Roman Road" method. The Book of Romans was written by Paul to help non-Jewish people understand their need to become Christians. Four verses found in Romans show how to receive Jesus as Lord and Savior.

Tell that person:
1. *"All have sinned and fall short of the glory of God"* (Romans 3:23). At some time in your life you have sinned against God. This sin now separates you from God's presence.

2. *"The wages of sin is death, but the gift of God is eternal life in Christ Jesus our Lord"* (Romans 6:23). The result of sin is death and eternal separation from God.

3. *"God demonstrates his own love for us in this: While we were still sinners, Christ died for us"* (Romans 5:8). Jesus died, not for his own sins, but for the sins you committed. You must believe Jesus' death and resurrection bought your salvation.

4. *"If you confess with your mouth, 'Jesus is Lord,' and believe in your heart that God raised him from the dead, you will be saved. For it is with your heart that you believe and are justified, and it is with your mouth that you confess and are saved"* (Romans 10:9-10). No one can accept salvation for you but yourself. It's your responsibility to pray and accept Jesus as your personal Savior.

A second, simpler method is the "ABC" plan. Have the person
    A: Admit he's a sinner (Romans 3:10).
    B: Believe on Jesus Christ (Acts 16:31).
    C: Confess his sin to God, and confess God's lordship to
       others (I John 1:9 and 4:15).

A person who receives the Lord should be told his name is now written in the "Book of Life," and upon his death he will live in the presence of the Lord Jesus forever. He needs to know he is now a "new creature in Christ;" he has been bought with a price (Jesus' blood), and is no longer his own. Share Luke 2:52 with your new convert and explain how he has a responsibility to grow as Jesus did, in wisdom, stature, and favor with God and men. Leading people to Christ can be exciting and rewarding spiritual work. Those who lead others to Jesus are wise (Daniel 12:3).

Ministry to Christians:
"(we will give) our attention to prayer and the ministry of the word" (Acts 6:4). As a Noble Woman, you shouldn't limit your ministry to evangelism. After you discover your spiritual gift, use it for the Church.

As you deepen your relationship with God, you will realize the need to develop your personal ministry within a local church. How do you find your gift or discover which ministry best utilizes your talent? Some women already have a strong inclination of what their gift is; it can be a special talent or something they enjoy doing at home, work or church. Most Christians are naturally drawn into the ministries of a church which use their gifts. Sometimes, though, a person can be motivated by guilt or the misguided suggestions of others. As a result, they'll work in a ministry or variety of ministries in which they don't particularly excel. A Noble Woman takes time to develop a lifelong ministry. The Noble Woman of the Bible was careful to use her talent first for her own family, then for others. Don't allow your gift to become more important than the needs of your family or the other areas of your growth.

IV-12

In I Corinthians 12:4-6 you will find many ways to serve the Lord and minister to the people of your church. Just as your body is made of four parts (mental, physical, spiritual, and social) so too, the Body of Christ has several parts (verses 12-14). In fact, the gifts of the Holy Spirit listed in I Corinthians 12 can be categorized as to which area of growth they minister.

"Word of wisdom," *"word of knowledge,"* and *"faith"* are gifts which bless the **mental** (wisdom) side. The *"word of knowledge"* is a revelation from God of specific facts (not learned from any other source) to be used in helping others. *"Word of wisdom"* enables a Christian to apply the knowledge God has given him to general direction for another Christian's life. The *"gift of faith,"* unlike normal spiritual faith, which is a fruit of the spirit, is an extraordinary faith given to a Christian for specific purposes, and at specific times.

Gifts pertaining to the physical side of the body include *"healing,"* *"miracles"* (anything physical accomplished supernaturally), and *"prophecy"* (identifying sin which involves the flesh). The spiritual gifts are *"discernment,"* *"speaking in unknown languages,"* and *"interpretation of languages."* *"Discernment"* is the Christian's ability to sense whether another person is influenced by a demonic spirit or the Spirit of God. *"Speaking in unknown languages,"* commonly referred to as *"tongues,"* can give a Christian the ability to witness to an unbeliever in his native language without prior knowledge of that language. This gift is also what Paul referred to when he stated his spirit often prayed with groans and utterings he couldn't understand. It's a way of communicating with God spirit-to-spirit and edifies the believer. The gift of *"interpretation"* is the ability to make sense out of the unknown languages spoken.

God has an appointed ministry for everyone in the Church. These ministries fall into the social area of growth. Every Christian should be involved in one of these seven ministries as part of his spiritual service to God. They include the ministry of *"witnessing,"* *"prophecy,"* *"teaching,"* working *"miracles,"* *"healing,"* *"helps"* or service, *"administration"* and encouragement. These ministries are the reason churches large enough have the practical services of a food bank, the encouraging ministry of a drama group, and the spiritual ministry of a prayer chain.

The purpose of the Church is to serve the saints (I Corinthians 16:15). Are you devoted to those in your church? The Holy Spirit directs people to the ministry God wants them to provide. If you have difficulty placing yourself, read over the list of gifts of the Holy Spirit. Ask the Lord to direct you to the spiritual work

He wants to place in your hands. Sometimes the best way to find your gift is to offer yourself over a period of months or years to several or all ministries in your church until you find the one which is most fulfilling and joyous to you. Remember to serve the Lord with gladness (Psalm 100:2) and *"see to it that you complete the work you have received in the Lord"* (Colossians 4:17).

SUMMARY

The Noble Woman wants to grow in favor with God and one day hear Him say, "Well done, thou good and faithful servant." God wants His servants to be doers of His Word (James 1:22). Follow the example of the Noble Woman. Discover the gift the Holy Spirit has given you. You need to be a witness for Jesus. *"However, I consider my life worth nothing to me, if only I may finish the race and complete the task the Lord Jesus has given me — the task of testifying to the gospel of God's grace"* (Acts 20:24). After spending time with God alone it's equally important to serve others, both Christian and non-Christian.

"Therefore, since through God's mercy we have this ministry, we do not lose heart" (II Corinthians 4:1). Growing in favor with God by serving the saints and being a witness is satisfying and keeps the Christian life from becoming dull. Sharing Christ with a non-Christian is an honor you shouldn't take lightly. God trusts you to be His witness on earth. There's no greater privilege than to minister to a group of Christians in a church-family setting.

ASSIGNMENT

There are no new verses to memorize this week. Use this chance to review verses from previous lessons. If you've fallen behind in the assignments, dedicate yourself to memorizing all the verses. It may be difficult to catch up, but don't give up. Review Proverbs 3:1-20 and Romans 6.

Suggestion: *"Commit to the Lord whatever you do, and your plans will succeed"* (Proverbs 16:3). To memorize Scripture you must be committed. Set time aside daily for review. Incorporate learning new verses into your daily lifestyle; it must become a way of life, not a temporary, unnatural exercise.

Lesson 13
Why Pray?

IV-13

PURPOSE

To learn what prayer is, why you should pray, and how to get prayers answered.

OVERVIEW

Why pray? Should prayer be a way of life for the average Christian? If so, what kind of prayer life should a Noble Woman have? Jesus expects you to pray. He gave much instruction to His disciples concerning prayer. His disciples, noticing the wonderful relationship Jesus had with the Father, asked Jesus to teach them how to pray. All Christians are expected to deepen their relationship with God through prayer. *"They all joined together constantly in prayer, along with the women and Mary the mother of Jesus, and his brothers"* (Acts 1:14). An active prayer life goes hand-in-hand with witnessing and ministering to the saints. What's a prayer life all about? How many definitions does prayer have? If you want to become a Noble Woman you must learn how to satisfy Jesus' command to pray.

Prayer involves two parts. It's communication between two individuals — you and God. Your part in prayer involves sharing your heart, the claims you make in spiritual authority and the requests you make to the Sovereign God. God's part is listening to you, responding with love and guidance, and sending out angels to answer your prayer requests. If you spend time speaking to God but not listening, you only accomplish half of prayer's purpose.

Often, Christians pray for years wondering if, or when, their prayers will be heard or answered by God. This lesson will teach you how to be sure God will answer your prayers. You'll take a close look at God's will concerning your prayer life. Sometimes Christians pray for a long period of time about something only to give up before the answer comes. The discussion will offer words of encouragement and teach you to apply God's Word in receiving your prayer requests. Finally, it will look at the example of another Noble Woman in the Bible (Hannah), and the secret to the prophet Elijah's powerful prayer life. Hannah's prayer and request in I Samuel was both unusual and common, personal and world changing. It's an excellent prayer to examine. Elijah repeatedly prayed for life-changing miracles. He was never afraid to boast his prayers would be answered. How can a Noble Woman emulate both Hannah's desperation and Elijah's assurance that God will answer unusual and powerful prayer requests?

DISCUSSION

Why pray? Perhaps a better question for a Noble Woman is, "Why don't I pray?" Every Christian true to his faith will readily admit God wants and expects him to pray. What better reason could there be than, "God wants me to"? The second question is harder to answer. "Why don't I pray if it's what God wants me to do?" The devil will do everything he can to keep you from praying. You're most powerful when on your knees. Prayer, indeed, is spiritual warfare. It's a battle between your spirit and the powers of darkness; it's hard work. Your power over Satan increases in direct proportion to the amount you pray; even hell can't prevail against you (Matthew 16:18). However, a selfish nature *can* keep you from prayer. If you harbor sin in your heart it's difficult to come before the Almighty God in prayer. Don't confuse this, however, with guilt the devil will use to keep you from prayer. Sin can be confessed and cleansed from you; guilt, which continues to plague you after God forgives past sin, has no basis for keeping you from feeling righteous under the blood of Jesus. There's no reason to keep sin unconfessed and hinder your prayer life. Another kind of sin which stops your prayer life from reaching its full potential is selfishness. In its advanced stages prayer is totally unselfish. It's concerned with the needs of others, compassionate and sorrowful over people uncommitted to Christ, and especially concerned for people who haven't yet received Christ or haven't yet heard the precious name of Jesus.

In order to pray you must know what prayer is. Prayer is working up a spiritual sweat. It includes a spectrum of activities. Prayer is worship, coming before the presence of God. It's asking and listening. It's standing in the gap and speaking words of life (Bible verses) over someone's situation. It's bringing a need before the King of kings. It's asking your daddy for a present. Prayer is standing with the angels in their fight against demonic forces. Prayer is putting your belief into action. Jesus, Himself, tells us, *"If thou canst believe, all things are possible to him that believeth"* (Mark 9:23 KJV). Prayer can be a conversation between two people who love each other. The way to "pray without ceasing" is to carry on an all day conversation with God.

"Do not be anxious about anything, but in everything by prayer and petition, with thanksgiving, present your requests to God" (Philippians 4:6). Prayer is God's answer to worry. Prayer is a **lifestyle** for a spiritual Christian. Prayer is meeting the point of your belief. *"Therefore I tell you, whatever you ask for in prayer, believe that you have received it, and it will be yours"* (Mark 11:24). Prayer is forgiveness. You know God forgives you through confession; but you are to forgive others when you pray (Mark 11:25). Prayer is opening the door to the spiritual realm and doing battle on the front lines. Jesus has given you the authority, exercised by prayer, to break the bonds of the enemy and claim his captives for the kingdom of God.

When you meet God in prayer, each has a part to perform. God does His part first. He draws you, by His Holy Spirit, to communicate with Him. He has proven repeatedly throughout the Bible that He doesn't lie. He will accomplish His Word and do whatever He has promised to do. God's part is doing the actual work of your prayers. He sees to it an answer comes. He draws people to salvation in answer to your prayers, and He's the One who saves them. He provides for your needs. He teaches you about His kingdom and the use of authority. He heals you. He shows pleasure and positive response when you praise Him. But His part isn't accomplished without your part. *"And ye shall seek me, and find me, when ye shall search for me with all your heart"* (Jeremiah 29:13 KJV). Your part is to do the seeking. He has promised to do His part by giving you anything when you do your part by obeying His commands and doing what pleases Him (I John 3:22). He does His part by giving you power over the enemy (Luke 10:19), but you must do your part in binding evil on earth. *"Verily I say unto you, Whatsoever ye shall bind on earth shall be bound in Heaven: and whatsoever ye shall loose on earth shall be loosed in Heaven. Again I say unto you, that if two of you shall agree on earth as touching anything that they shall ask, it shall be done for them of my Father which is in Heaven"* (Matthew 18:18-19 KJV). God will do His part and deliver you out of trouble when you do your part in prayer and call out to Him (Psalm 50:15). The most important part in prayer is faith. The element of faith in prayer is truly your own. The words you pray aren't necessarily your own. Paul tells us we don't know how to pray; we often don't have the words. The Holy Spirit must tell us what to say. We certainly don't have the desire to pray, so God must give us that desire and motivate us with His promises. Of course the results of prayer aren't our own. Although prayer changes things, it's God who does the changing. So, what you truly have to offer prayer is your own faith. *"According to your faith be it unto you"* (Matthew 9:29 KJV).

Victory:

"The Lord is not slack concerning his promise, as some men count slackness; but is long suffering to usward, not willing that any should perish, but that all should come to repentance" (II Peter 3:9 KJV). *"Let us not become weary in doing good, for at the proper time we will reap a harvest if we do not give up"* (Galatians 6:9). You gain victory through prayer, not by finding a perfect formula for asking or believing, but by not giving up before you receive the answer. In addition, there are certain steps you must take to assure victory in prayer:

1. **Confess all sin.** *"If I regard iniquity in my heart, the Lord will not hear me"* (Psalm 66:18 KJV). *"But your iniquities have separated between you and your God and your sins have hid His face from you, that He will not hear"* (Isaiah 59:2 KJV). The seven most powerful sins that may go unconfessed are pride, covetousness, lust, anger, gluttony, envy, and sloth. Of these, pride is easily undetected and deceitfully entraps you. God resists the pray-er who is proud (James 4:6-7). Proverbs 116:18 KJV says, *"Pride goeth before destruction, and a haughty spirit before a fall."* The way to avoid this is to confess all sin and ask God to reveal any unconfessed sin. *"If we confess our sins, He is faithful and just to forgive us our sins, and to cleanse us from all unrighteousness"* (I John 1:9 KJV).

2. **Forgive all offenders.** *"And when you stand praying, if you hold anything against anyone, forgive him, so that your Father in heaven may forgive you your sins"* (Mark 11:25). This isn't only so your own sin may be forgiven but so your offerings of praise to God will be acceptable (Matthew 5:23). When you forgive others for

offending you, God forgives you. You'll see new victory in your answered prayers.

3. **Know God's Word.** *"And take the helmet of salvation, and the sword of the Spirit, which is the word of God"* (Ephesians 6:17). If you know God's Word, you know God's will and what to ask for in prayer. *"If we ask anything according to His will, He heareth us"* (I John 5:14 KJV). If your prayers aren't being answered, perhaps the reason is yourself rather than any failure on God's part. *"Ye ask and receive not because ye ask amiss, that ye may consume it upon your lusts"* (James 4:3 KJV).

4. **Praise God for everything.** Do you let your requests be made known with thanksgiving? Praise is a part of prayer many Christians forget. Without it a prayer life withers and eventually dies. *"I will praise thee for ever, because thou hast done it: and I will wait on thy name; for it is good before thy saints"* (Psalm 52:9 KJV). *"I will praise thee: for thou hast heard me"* (Psalm 118:21 KJV). Praise was a powerful ally for Paul and Silas. When they added it to prayer, they were released from prison bonds (Acts 16). When you reach a point where you are able to praise God for anything and thank Him for everything, you will have added power to your prayers.

5. **Know the power of Jesus.** It's because of Jesus you're able to ask the Father for anything. Jesus told the disciples numerous times, especially in the Book of John, that praying in His name will bring results (John 14:13 and 14; John 15:16; John 16:23). You're given "power of attorney" through the name of Jesus. In Jesus' name you can cast out demons, heal the sick, or move mountains. His name is above any other name. *"The name of the Lord is a strong tower"* (Proverbs 18:10 KJV). The cross and the blood also bring victory to spiritual warfare. *"And they overcame him by the blood of the Lamb and by the word of their testimony; and they loved not their lives unto the death"* (Revelation 12:11 KJV).

6. **Build your faith.** Building your faith with the promises of the Scriptures can add support to a sagging prayer life. The New Testament, from Matthew to Revelation, is filled with uplifting words which will build your faith. You need faith to move mountains, faith to ask and believe without wavering. *"So I say to you: Ask and it will be given to you; seek and you will find; knock and the door will be opened to you. For everyone who asks receives; he who seeks finds; and to him who knocks, the door will be opened"* (Luke 11:9-10). If your prayers aren't answered because you just don't believe it's possible, refer to these faith-building Scriptures. You can have all your desires and needs met, including mental, physical, spiritual, and social (I Corinthians 1:7; I Corinthians 3:21-22; II Corinthians 5:7; II Corinthians 9:8; Ephesians 3:12; Philippians 4:19; I Thessalonians 5:24; Philemon 1:6; Hebrews 1:14; James 1:5; I Peter 2:24). If you have doubts about your authority over forces of evil, read and meditate over these verses: John 15:7; Acts 13:39; Romans 5:17; Ephesians 3:16; Ephesians 3:20; Philippians 4:13; II Thessalonians 3:3; Hebrews 2:8; Hebrews 12:28; Hebrews 13:21; I Peter 1:5. *"His divine power has given us everything we need for life and godliness through our knowledge of him who called us by his own glory and goodness. Through these he has given us his very great and precious promises, so*

that through them you may participate in the divine nature and escape the corruption in the world caused by evil desires" (II Peter 1:3-4).

7. **Have a Christ-centered life.** The balanced life of a Noble Woman, one who grows in all four areas, is simply a life centered on Jesus Christ. Pattern yourself after Him in all ways. *"I am the vine; you are the branches. If a man remains in me and I in him, he will bear much fruit; apart from me you can do nothing"* (John 15:5). To gain total victory in your prayer life, submit to Jesus in everything. Live your life "in the spirit" (Ephesians 5:18). When you submit to God you won't limit Him as to how He must answer your prayers. Limiting God puts constraints on your prayers and leaves you unsatisfied. *"For though we walk in the flesh, we do not war after the flesh: (For the weapons of our warfare are not carnal, but mighty through God to the pulling down of strongholds); casting down imaginations, and every high thing that exalteth itself against the knowledege of God, and bringing into captivity every thought to the obedience of Christ"* (II Corinthians 10:3-5 KJV).

It doesn't matter how many times you've tried to gain victory in your prayer life before; go over these steps again and again and victory will come. God will remain true to His promise if you don't give up.

IV-13

Hannah:

"In those days Israel had no king; everyone did as he saw fit" (Judges 21:25). The days of Hannah's Israel were exemplified by self-centeredness and anarchy. Even the priest Eli's sons were careless ungodly leaders of the people. The national situation for Israel was grim. The strong Philistines were neighbors. In this depressive, barren country setting Hannah made a prayer request to her God. Hannah's life was an emotional roller coaster. She was loved deeply by her husband and despised by her husband's other wife. Hannah suffered from the stigma of being unable to bear children. Although this didn't bother her husband, Elkanah, the rest of society shunned Hannah. The other wife, who had children herself, taunted Hannah about her childless condition. Hannah needed consolation and a way out of her shame so she went to her God. *"In bitterness of soul Hannah wept much and prayed to the Lord. And she made a vow, saying, 'O Lord Almighty, if you will only look upon your servant's misery and remember me, and not forget your servant but give her a son, then I will give him to the Lord for all the days of his life, and no razor will ever be used on his head'"* (I Samuel 1:10-11). This was an interesting and brave prayer for a woman to make at that time in history. Although it was normal to refer to herself as a servant of the Lord and to ask God for a son, making a vow was a sacred and bold thing for a woman to do. In addition, she called God "Jehovah Sabaoth," which is translated "Lord of Hosts." She used a higher name for God; she addressed the all-powerful God, the One who had the power to change even a barren woman. Hannah promised God she'd raise her son according to the Nazarite vow and would not cut his hair, a symbol which would mark him as a servant of God. She did all this without consulting her husband.

Hannah used a type of prayer known as supplication, characterized by groans and deep grieving. She prayed so hard her lips moved but no sound came out. The priest Eli didn't recognize her deep praying. He mistook her for a drunk. After she heard the priest pray for her (verse 17) she went away with new hope and faith. Before she even received an answer from God she worshipped Him (verse 19). After all those years of waiting for a child, her prayers were finally answered. She received the son she'd always wanted. She held that most precious baby in her arms and nursed him with care. After two or three short years of pouring herself into little Samuel's life, she took him to the temple to be raised for God.

Hannah was true to her vow to God. What was the result? For her, personally, the result was added blessing. Hannah conceived three sons and two daughters. Samuel became the prophet of Israel (I Samuel 2:21); but Samuel's being given to God had an even greater effect on the nation. Because of the prophet Samuel, Israel had godly leadership and received her first King, Saul, who unified the nation against the Philistines. Samuel also anointed and chose David to be king and bring a new era of victory and, eventually, peace to Israel. Why would God allow a barren Hannah to cry out to Him for so long before He answered her prayer? Could it be God had a greater purpose than just giving her a son? It's possible He wanted Hannah to be desperate enough for a baby that she would make a vow to give her first son to God. In your prayer life God is behind the scenes constantly working according to His plan. He's waiting to hear you ask for the very things He wants to give you. Hannah sang a song of praise to God after Samuel was born. She recognized the majesty of God's power to answer prayer. *"For the foundations of the earth are the Lord's; upon them he has set the world. He will guard the feet of his saints"* (I Samuel 2:8-9).

Elijah:

James 5:13-19 reveals the power behind prayers of faith. Prayer is the answer James gives to Christians who are troubled, happy, sick, or sinning. *"The effectual fervent prayer of a righteous man availeth much"* (James 5:16 KJV). James tells you that when you realize you're righteous in God's eyes (Romans 6) you'll gain new boldness and power in your prayers; you'll strive to know the will of God, pray accordingly and render your prayers effective. Sound familiar? These are the same steps to victory you've been studying. Following his discussion on prayer, James mentions Elijah, saying this great man of prayer was just like everyone else (verse 17).

How could that be? Elijah was a man who suffered from the fears of ungodly people. He sometimes got tired of doing God's will. What enabled him to believe God for miracles in his life? He knew God's Word. He continued to persevere in his prayers because he knew God had already willed the answers. The prophet Elijah knew the Pentateuch. Deuteronomy 11:17 warned that if the people worshipped other gods, the Lord would stop the rain long enough for the crops to dry up. Elijah knew the conditions of that verse applied to his situation. He knew God's response would be favorable when he prayed for the rain to stop for three years.

When the rain stopped, however, Elijah's prayer wasn't over. He continued to seek God's will and **listen** to God so he would know when the rain should come again (I Kings 18:1). Did you detect Elijah's secret to answered prayer? He prayed according to God's Word as he knew it. He, and Hannah too, persevered until the answer came. They both prayed with intensity. They opened their prayer lives to include the needs of their people.

IV-13

SUMMARY

Why pray? Most importantly, because Jesus tells you to pray (Matthew 6:6). He said you should always pray and not give up on your requests (Luke 18:1). Peter, one of the disciples closest to Jesus, also said to pray (Acts 8:24). In I Corinthians 14, Paul too said to pray. You should pray because God has promised to hear you (Jeremiah 33:3; I Kings 9:3; II Chronicles 7:14; Isaiah 58:9; Zechariah 13:9, I Peter 3:12). You should pray because you are an ambassador for Christ to the unsaved (II Corinthians 5:20), and a concerned brother to the saved (Galatians 6:2).

Yield to God's attempts to draw you to prayer. Grow in favor with God. Build you faith with the promises in His Word. You shouldn't limit the power, the will, or the purpose of God in your prayers. The Holy Spirit constantly calls you to deeper prayer. You haven't begun to enter into the throne room of God; to see and believe His Sovereignty. God has much to offer in a life of prayer. He wants to open doors for you.

Think of prayer as a spiritual body-building exercise. You won't be a Charles Atlas overnight. The longer and harder you pray, the stronger the pray-er you will be. Remember, prayer is the best teacher of prayer. Start where you are; don't wait until you totally understand prayer. You may never get started! Don't intimidate yourself by comparing your prayer life to another's. Your relationship to God is different from anyone else's and your prayer life reflects that. There's not only one correct way to pray. God isn't in heaven saying, "No, no, you didn't go through the correct steps. Start over or forget it." Instead God looks into your heart and knows your intention; He overlooks any blind spots in order to accommodate your prayers as they align themselves with His Word. He's quick to give you all you ask for that doesn't go against His Word. God is for you, not against you. Notice in your own life how He answers prayers that align themselves to His Word.

The lifeline for a Noble Woman is a strong prayer life. This important element added to your devotional life brings power and effectiveness to any spiritual work for God. Prayer brings you into favor with God.

ASSIGNMENT

Begin memorizing Scripture again by adding Proverbs 3:21-24. Have you noticed how each area of growth overlaps the other? For instance, in your memory work you learn wisdom helps you sleep better. As you grow in one of the four areas, you're also able to grow in the others — if you lead a life of submission to God.

Suggestion: *"How sweet are your promises to my taste, sweeter than honey to my mouth"* (Psalm 119:103). Think of eating great food when you memorize God's Word. Every verse is like a meal, each word a bite. Chew on each bite. Use this idea to remind yourself to practice memory verses before and after each meal. Keep a 3 x 5 Scripture card in your silverware drawer. Set it at your place at the table during mealtime.

Lesson 14
How to Pray

IV-14

PURPOSE
To learn how to pray and what the Bible says to pray for.

OVERVIEW
Learning how to pray is a major step in a Noble Woman's life. Once you've learned the basics of prayer you can move into a deeper prayer life. Prayer is a business which is never exhausted. With prayer you can touch anyone and everyone's life. You can cause miracles to happen in people's lives. The Bible is specific about who and what to pray for. As a pray-er you should know what comprises an adequate prayer list. The need can seem endless. Where do you stop? The task can seem so great you may also ask, "Where do you begin?" This lesson takes a look at everything which could be included in your prayer time.

DISCUSSION
Your prayer life should be such that your daily life leads you to prayer, and your prayers affect your daily life. One builds upon the other until your prayer life grows as you grow in wisdom, stature, and favor with God and men. Your relationship to the entire world will change. As you grow spiritually you'll find more to pray about. When you begin your prayer time, remember to prepare your mind and heart. *"Do not conform any longer to the pattern of this world, but be transformed by the renewing of your mind. Then you will be able to test and approve what God's will is — his good, pleasing and perfect will"* (Romans 12:2). Isn't that what you want to discover in prayer — God's perfect will? The Bible describes different forms of prayer. In reality, the ways to pray are as varied as the individuals who pray. The Bible does mention particular kinds of prayer; it would benefit your personal prayer life to understand each to the best of your ability and incorporate them into your prayer life.

Kinds of Prayer

1. **Confession.** The first few minutes of your prayer time should be spent in confession, renewing your mind. Make yourself holy before God in order to approach Him in prayer. Wash yourself with the Word by confessing any sin that has come between you and God or you and others (Ephesians 5:26-27). After submitting to God, by confession, you gain authority to resist the devil and make him flee. This is an important phase of prayer. *"Submit yourselves, then, to God. Resist the devil, and he will flee from you. Come near to God and he will come near to you"* (James 4:7-8). You need to banish the devil at the start of your prayer time, before he distracts you from the work of serious prayer.

2. **Praise.** As soon as you have confessed any sin in your life and

felt His purifying cleansing, you're ready to enter His courts with praise. Praise has miraculous power. Don't wait until you "feel" like praising God to worship Him, or the devil will see to it you never "feel" like it. The Bible says many times to praise, worship, glorify, and be thankful to God in everything and for everything. There is never a condition of "feelings" put on this command. You praise Him in obedience to His command. Praise is a sacrifice to God. Offer up praise to God sacrificing any feelings you have at the time. Psalm 63, as well as most of the Psalms, is a beautiful expression of praise. Verse 3 says, *"My lips will glorify you,"* indicating we should open our mouths and praise out loud. Another part of praise is the position of your hands. *"I will praise you as long as I live, and in your name I will lift up my hands"* (verse 4). Lifting your hands to God is a sign of submission and desire; it's the child reaching out to its parent; it's a heart opening up; it's a realization of who you are and who God is. *"With singing lips my mouth will praise you"* (verse 5). Singing is a part of praise. Sing to God during prayer and joy will well up within your soul. You'll feel the comfort of God. This is excellent preparation for requests made later in your prayer time. Singing God's praises makes you confident He will hear you. The Psalms were originally set to music. Any Scripture can be sung to God; you can make up a song in your heart. God will delight in that as much as you delight in hearing your own children's made-up songs. A great reason for adding praise to your prayer time is the benefit of joy. Praise brings joy; joy brings strength. Thus, you'll have strength for the rest of your prayer time as well as for the rest of your day.

3. **Thanksgiving.** As praise is rejoicing in the giver, thanksgiving is rejoicing in the gift. *"Let them give thanks to the Lord for his unfailing love and his wonderful deeds for men. Let them sacrifice thank offerings and tell of his works with songs of joy"* (Psalm 107:21-22). Praise and thanksgiving go hand-in-hand but are always mentioned as separate parts of prayer. Being thankful for what you have received from God (which includes every good thing in your life) and thanking Him for what He continues to bless you with in your life keeps your possessions consecrated and doctrinally pure (I Timothy 4:4). Praise and thanksgiving are good introductions to petition.

4. **Petition.** Petition is a personal request you make of God for yourself or others. It's not so much **who** you're praying for as **what.** This is the list of daily needs you ask God to give you. Jesus petitioned God in the "Our Father" when He asked for daily bread, and not to be lead into temptation. These were specific requests. It's best to be specific with God when making requests. Ask God for a needed pair of shoes, for instance, rather than "some money" to get the shoes. God is very good at honoring detail, as you are when your children request specific things for Christmas. You want them to be specific. You want to know exactly what they want so you can make them happy. So it is with your heavenly Father. *"And if we know that he hears us, whatsoever we ask, we know that we have the petitions that we desired of him"* (I John 5:15 KJV). Your petitions, or specific requests, aren't to be confined to yourself. Ephesians 6:18 makes it clear you're to make petitions for all the saints. You should

pray for the needs of your fellow Christians, asking specifically for them, too.

5. **Intercession.** According to the dictionary, the term "intercession," or its root, "intercede," is a form of mediating between two parties for reconciliation. Lift up the names of others before God asking Him to shed His favor and blessing upon them. Instead of asking for needs, as in petition, pray for the person directly and somewhat generally. Jesus was your intercessor when He mediated between your sin and God's judgment on the cross. *"He saw that there was no one, and he was appalled that there was no one to intercede; so his own arm worked salvation for him"* (Isaiah 59:16). He continues to intercede on your behalf. He's the example to remember when interceding for others during your prayer time. During His life on earth Jesus constantly lifted up His disciples and future disciples to God that they might have His blessing. *"Therefore he (Jesus) is able to save completely those who come to God through Him, because he always lives to intercede for them"* (Hebrews 7:25).

IV-14

Intercession is praying for others who don't know how to pray for themselves. This is definitely true for non-Christians. Believers, too, sometimes have difficulty seeing their situation from God's perspective or have somehow blocked their ability to pray to God for themselves. God's nature is such that He doesn't enter a person's life without being invited. It's up to you to invite Jesus to work in someone else's life. Don't dismiss this responsibility lightly. People often come to God because someone has prayed for them consistently for months or years. The Holy Spirit also intercedes for you when you don't know how to pray (Romans 8:26). Allow Him to express Himself in your prayer life, with a prayer language, when you don't know how to pray.

6. **Supplication.** This isn't a regular part of daily prayer but you should be familiar with it and listen to God for times He wants you to accomplish some great prayer work through supplication. This kind of prayer moves the very hand of God. It involves intensity, begging, pleading, or imploring God to answer a specific cause. It's usually connected with urgency (as in a couple about to declare divorce, an immediate medical emergency, or a great financial burden). It can also mean the difference in a true revival in a local church, a world-changing crisis, or a life-threatening situation. It's part of the strongest spiritual battle and is often accompanied by fasting. A supplicant of the court, from which the term "supplication" is derived, was a person who would throw himself on the mercy of the court asking earnestly and humbly to have the guilty party (whether himself or another) totally pardoned. This was the case when Moses pleaded in supplication to God for the entire nation of Israel.

What happened to the Israelites as they came out of Egypt and wandered in the wilderness is an almost unbelievable story. In many ways their story is symbolic of what happens to Christians. First of all God saved them in a miraculous way (ten plagues, ending with the deaths of the first born sons of Egyptians) from a life of horrible slavery. Moses lead them to a land of their own, a beautiful place to be free and multiply into a strong nation. God showed them special favor, but the people became nervous when they saw the Egyptian army coming after them in full force. God understood their feelings and wasn't about to let them down. He helped the Israelites cross the Red Sea and destroyed the Egyptian army. The Israelites didn't have to fight one soldier! When they complained about their diet God daily provided food and more meat than they could eat. He invited Moses to meet with Him on Mt. Sinai and directed the people to wait for instructions. Not once had God failed them. He'd always taken care of them; he'd always come through with what He promised. He said He was going to speak to Moses and then Moses would come down and speak to them. They were supposed to wait, and obey God's laws. What did they do! They got tired of waiting for Moses (it had been forty days) and disobeyed God by making a golden calf to worship. Needless to say, God was upset. He was so upset He was ready to destroy His entire nation and start over with Moses. Moses, doubtless because he'd just spent forty days getting to know God's heart, didn't want to see this happen. He prayed to God in supplication on behalf of the nation of Israel. He didn't want to see God's witness in the world ruined as a result of God killing His own people. Moses plead his case. The Bible states simply, *"Then the Lord relented and did not bring his people the disaster he had threatened"* (Exodus 32:14).

7. **Listening.** The last part of your prayer time should be spent listening to God. Up to this point you've been the only one communicating in prayer; now it's God's turn. He wants to speak to your heart. Don't expect a voice from the sky or a visitation from a "heavenly being" (although it's been known to happen), but rather be content with the well-being in your spirit that will come from the tender voice of God telling you He loves you. *"I pray that out of his glorious riches he may strengthen you with power through his Spirit in your inner being, so that Christ may dwell in your hearts through faith. And I pray that you, being rooted and established in love, may have power, together with all the saints, to grasp how wide and long and high and deep is the love of Christ"* (Ephesians 3:16-18). This part of prayer is reminiscent of the story of the Lord appearing to Elijah. God wasn't in the great wind, the earthquake, or the fire, but in a gentle whisper (I Kings 19:12).

What to Pray For:

1. **Anything.** The first thing to remember to ask God for is: anything. Jesus repeatedly told His disciples they could ask for anything in prayer. *"Whatsoever ye shall ask in my Name, that will I do. If ye shall ask anything in my Name, I will do it"* (John 14:13-14 KJV). Anything and everything can be the subject of prayer. God wants you to feel free to ask Him for anything good you desire. He's the giver of all good things (John 16:23; Luke 18:1; I Thessalonians 5:17).

2. **Government leaders.** Even if you don't agree with the politics of your government and state leaders, you must submit to them and pray for them (Romans 13:1-4). If you rebel against them, you rebel against God. It's God who gives authority to rule. *"I urge, then, first of all, that requests, prayers, intercession and thanksgiving be made for everyone — for kings and all those in authority, that we may live peaceful and quiet lives in all godliness and*

holiness. This is good, and pleases God" (I Timothy 2:1-3). Pray the leaders are open to evangelism in their countries, that they won't be oppressive to the people, and that miracles will exist as a way of establishing God's witness.

3. Missionaries and their families. Most missionaries are highly neglected by the very people who should be supporting them in daily prayer. No one fights on the front line of spiritual battle more than a missionary and his family. The Gospel of Christ precludes the existence of missionaries. If a Christian isn't willing to be a missionary himself, he should take every opportunity to support a missionary work. Adopt a missionary group or family in a country which sparks your interest. Provide time in your daily prayers to lift up specific needs of this missionary. A good pattern to follow when praying for missionaries is to cover all four areas of growth. Pray for the missionary's needs for:

a. wisdom: learning the language, having an open heart for cultural differences.

b. stature: adaption to food, ability to sleep, strength for new physical demands, and excellent health.

c. favor with God: strong devotional time, direction from God in the work, faith for miracles.

d. favor with men: acclimation to new customs, strong family unit, ability and help in training their children, many strong Christian friends to fellowship with, and submission to mission board and local church.

4. Workers for God's work. *"Then he said to his disciples, 'The harvest is plentiful but the workers are few. Ask the Lord of the harvest, therefore, to send out workers into his harvest field'"* (Matthew 9:37-38). We often pray in reverse order. We spend much time praying for people to come to God and ignore the need for Christians to go tell these people about God. How can they know, except they hear from someone? We should spend more time praying for Christians to be bold about witnessing and sharing the Gospel.

5. Enemies. One of the hardest verses in Scripture to obey is Matthew 5:44, *"But I tell you: Love your enemies and pray for those who persecute you, that you may be sons of your Father in heaven."* What's your first reaction when someone hurts you in some way? You want to reject them or revenge the wrong. But God wants you to pray for them and see them through His eyes. Praying for your enemies is what distinguishes you from the world. Anyone can love someone who loves him back. It's loving those who despise you that makes you different. Praying for your enemies keeps you from allowing bitterness and unforgiveness to enter your life, rendering other prayers ineffective. Be sure to pray on a regular basis for people who have hurt you.

6. Knowledge and understanding of His will. *"For this reason, since the day we heard about you, we have not stopped praying for you and asking God to fill you with the knowledge of his will through all spiritual wisdom and understanding"* (Colossians 1:9). The constant prayer of a Noble Woman should be to have wisdom (James 1:5) and an open heart (Ephesians 1:18) in knowing

God's will. This results directly in growing in favor with God. Praying to know God's will in every area of your life helps keep the rest of your prayers focused on God.

7. **Help during trouble and perseverance during trials.** *"Is any one of you in trouble? He should pray"* (James 5:13). It's mentioned throughout Psalms that God is a help to those in trouble. He'll only work in your life when invited. God expects you to ask for help when you're in a difficult situation. James, chapter 1, describes many kinds of trials and what your attitude should be as you face trials in your life. God wants you to go through trials because they make you strong. His help is the perseverance to finish walking through the trials. *"Blessed is the man who perseveres under trial, because when he has stood the test, he will receive the crown of life that God has promised to those who love him"* (James 1:12). This should be a daily prayer concern.

8. **Healing.** The Book of James is a wealth of information on prayer. The need to pray for healing is mentioned in the Book of James. *"And the prayer offered in faith will make the sick person well; the Lord will raise him up. If he has sinned, he will be forgiven"* (James 5:15). Many people take medications every day for illness or health problems. Most people are involved in some kind of preventative medicine. Why shouldn't daily prayer be added to the list of health attention? You're told to pray for your own health as well as the health of others. You're told to pray for those who are sick or suffer disability or disease. You shouldn't question whether being sick or unhealthy is God's will; you've already been given direction in His Word to pray for the sick.

9. **Decisions.** When you have a decision to make in your life, seek God's will in prayer to be certain you're led by the Holy Spirit and not fleshly desires. You should try to view your circumstances from God's perspective. Don't rely on your own knowledge of the situation (Proverbs 3:6). Favorable circumstances don't imply God is leading through that door. Although He does want your joy to be complete, God doesn't want decisions based on personal pleasure or convenience to rule your life. Once you've determined God's will, through prayer, there should be no doubts clouding your commitment to obey God's will. Following through on a decision made by prayer is easy. God respects your desire to love Him completely and won't allow you to wander from His guiding hand.

10. **Desires.** Although they aren't to be your only request in prayer, God made provision for your desires as well as needs. *"Therefore I say unto you, What things soever ye desire, when ye pray, believe that ye receive them, and ye shall have them"* (Mark 11:24 KJV). He wants your heart to be satisfied. *"Delight thyself also in the Lord; and he shall give thee the desires of thine heart"* (Psalm 37:4 KJV).

SUMMARY

Jesus' words in Matthew 26:40-41 sum up what can be said about prayer. *"Could you not keep watch with me for one hour? . . . Watch and pray so that you will not fall into temptation. The spirit is willing, but the body is weak."* Prayer can be an exciting adventure or dry and lifeless; but it's always full of variety. Take advantage of all the forms of prayer, beginning with confession and praise, continuing with petition, intercession, supplication and finally, listening to God's response. Include everyone and everything God wants you to pray about on your prayer list.

There are other times to pray besides your devotional time with God. Prayer belongs in the Church, but it also belongs in fellowship. Pray with friends at the end of an evening together. Pray as soon as a need is mentioned so you won't forget. Prayer should be a part of mealtimes (I Timothy 4:4). A great use of time is to pray during "down time" — when standing in a grocery line, waiting at a traffic light, or in a doctor's office. There are needs everywhere. People desperately want an intercessor. Respond to prayer needs in your church as part of your ministry to God and your growth as a Noble Woman. You could be part of a missionary prayer band or prayer chain. Find a prayer partner who will lift you up daily in prayer as you pray for her. Prayer partners help make you responsible to pray, encourage you to share prayer burdens, and bring added power when to agree in Jesus' name. Be a prayer warrior for God and you will be a Noble Woman.

IV-14

ASSIGNMENT

Make yourself a prayer list. Use the information you've learned to include all areas of prayer discussed. Organize the list for daily or weekly prayer needs. Record your prayers. Date all answers you receive. Spend extra time this week in prayer. Ask God to teach you more about prayer.

TABLE 6

PRAY FOR ME

(By a Missionary)

Please pray for me, my friend, I need your prayers,
For there are burdens pressing hard and many cares.
Pray, too, that Christ will make of me
The Missionary that I ought to be.
Do for me, my friend, at morning hour,
That I may not be overborne by Satan's power.
That mid the whirl and maze of things,
My soul may drink of hidden springs.
And pray for me, my friend, when night comes on;
God's stars look down upon us both,
Apart . . . . Alone.
Will you, dear friend, before you sleep,
Pray Him, my Soul with yours to keep?
Cease not to pray for me, though sundered far,
Come, meet me at the mercy seat from where you are.
Nor time nor distance can divide
Our hearts that in HIS love abide,
Thus praying for each, that will come true,
Of which our Lord and Master spoke,
"If two of you . . ."

Lesson 15
Self-Evaluation E

PURPOSE

To discover your relationship to other people including your husband, children, parents, church members, friends, and neighbors. To observe any problems you might have in growing in favor with men.

OVERVIEW

Growing socially, in favor with men, is difficult for a Christian, and women in particular. As a Christian woman, you must redeem your time and not turn into a busybody or a gossip as you try to establish a close friendship. You must show wisdom and discretion in your compassion for others. You must be willing to give your expectations to God and let Him choose your friends. You must remember not to do anything for another person you haven't already done for your own family. You must submit to your husband and his desires for your life.

However, when you follow Biblical principles in taking care of your family, God will always provide a way for you to fulfill His will for you. This area of growth can make the strongest witness for Jesus. One of the mysteries Paul relates is of the godly marriage being a testimony that Jesus is real and is truly able to help Christians love each other as they should. When a husband and wife love, respect and submit to each other as God ordained, and train their children in Biblical principles, that family unit will affect more people than each member could have done individually.

The Noble Woman's relationship with everyone in her life affects her social growth. Don't neglect this area. Most Scripture deals with learning how to love others as God loves you. This final evaluation should help you put this area of your life in perspective with the others. Any personal problems revealed in your answers should be handled by allowing the Holy Spirit to work in your heart.

SELF-EVALUATION E

1. Describe your various kinds of friendships. Everyone has friends, or should have. Throughout your life you have gained

and lost friends for different reasons, become a friend to a different kind of person, or grown closer to a select group of people. Describe your friendships through the years. Explain your definition of a friendship. Describe how your friendships have changed since you became a Christian or grew closer to the Lord.

_____

_____

_____

_____

_____

_____

_____

_____

_____

2. Give a brief definition of these terms: acquaintance, casual friend, close friend, and special friend. What makes a special friend special? Do you classify your friends when you speak about them? Is it difficult for you to make one of these types of friendships? Why?

_____

_____

_____

_____

_____

_____

_____

_____

_____

3. Name one friend you have for each of the preceding terms. How has an acquaintance become more of a friend? When did a close friend become really special? How many special friends do you have? Do you have one best friend? How long have you known her? What makes her the best? If you have more than one special friend, describe why each is special. Have you always had a special friend in your life? How did that person become special to you?

_____

_____

_____

_____

_____

_____

_____

_____

4. Do you feel there's a type of friendship you lack? Do you develop more of one kind of friendship than another? Why? Do you have a hard time growing closer to acquaintances or casual friends? What stumbling blocks do you have in forming a certain kind of friendship?

_____

_____

_____

_____

_____

_____

_____

_____

_____

5. Do you have a plan for establishing friendships and causing them to grow? Who usually makes the first move in a friendship—you or the other person? Do you work at your friendships, or allow them to happen *naturally?* Are most of your friends from a particular area of your life, such as work or church? Do most of your friends know or get along well with your other friends? Are your friends separate from your husband's friends? Do you consider yourself to be friends with your husband?

_____

_____

_____

_____

_____

_____

_____

_____

6. List the different places you've met friends. Was it easier for you to make friends at one place over another? How much control do you think you have over who becomes your friend? Knowing where and how you make friends can reveal strengths and weaknesses in your personality. Growing in favor with men means developing all kinds of friendships with all kinds of people.

_____

_____

_____

_____

_____

_____

_____

_____

7. Do you attend a Bible-believing church at least once a week? Do you attend more often? Describe your church and why you attend as frequently as you do. One of God's commandments is to keep one day holy; but going to church is more than worshipping God; it's fellowship with people.

_____

_____

_____

_____

_____

_____

_____

_____

_____

V-15

8. How long have you been at your present church? A relationship to your church is similar to the one you have in marriage. First there's the honeymoon stage when everything at your church is wonderful. This is really strong if it's the church where you first became a Christian. You begin to think your local church is the most "spiritual" church there is; others just don't measure up; your church does everything in just the right way. Next comes a disillusionment stage when you discover your local church has its problems, mistakes, and sins. The church didn't change, your viewpoint did. Christians who don't recognize this stage for what it is think their church has lost its "spirituality." This is the time when most people leave their church for one they've heard is more "spiritual." They often repeat these stages at the next church, and so on. Those who stick with their church during the disillusionment phase find they reach a point where they accept the reality of the local church. Churches are composed of sinners with different relationships with Jesus. Learn to accept your church with its weaknesses, just as you want your church to accept you.

_____

_____

_____

_____

_____

_____

_____

_____

_____

9. List all the churches you have regularly attended and your reason for leaving each one. People who "church hop" do themselves and the rest of the Body of Christ a disservice. You can't visit church after church waiting to feel at home in one. You become attached to a church by attaching yourself to the people. You must give a church time. You must give God time to bring people into your life who need you or can fill your needs.

_____

_____

_____

_____

_____

_____

_____

_____

_____

10. Why do you attend your present church? What is it that drew you there? Are conditions the same now as when you first attended? Sometimes the reason God draws you isn't the reason He wants you to stay. Can you see how God worked behind the scenes in your life to place you in your church?

_____

_____

_____

_____

_____

_____

_____

_____

_____

11. In which church ministries do you participate? Why are you involved in each one? There are two main purposes for a ministry in a church. Either it ministers to those it is designed for or it ministers to and builds up the Christians who are involved in the ministry itself. A good ministry will do both. You could be drawn to a ministry for either of these main purposes. If you understand what attracted you, you won't become frustrated. If your desire is to minister to the people the ministry is designed for, stay away from ministries that contain a high amount of fellowship and emphasize group unity. If you're more interested in helping other Christians grow and forming strong friendships, stay in group-oriented ministries which encourage fellowship.

_____

_____

_____

_____

_____

_____

_____

_____

_____

V-15

12. Describe the local church's purpose as you see it. What purpose do you have in that local church? How much of the larger picture of the Body of Christ do you have? How do you help fulfill your church's purpose? Do you have friends from other churches?

_____

_____

_____

_____

_____

_____

_____

_____

_____

13. Describe the Body of Christ and what it means to you. Do you feel you're part of the Body of Christ? Is your church connected in any way with other churches? How? Does your church support missionaries? Do you know the missionaries your church supports?

_____

_____

_____

_____

_____

_____

_____

_____

_____

14. Briefly describe your strengths and weaknesses in your relationship with your husband and children. In your home you should be submissive to your husband. This doesn't mean you have no say, only that he has the **final** say. How well do you submit to him? The Bible doesn't put conditions on your submission. In other words, you can't wait for your husband to love you before you submit. This agrees with God's plan of giving before receiving. Do you put your children before your husband? (The best security you can give your children is to love your husband.) Children need to know what their limits are. They grow up trying to discover their limits by doing whatever their selfish natures desire until someone steps in and tells them "no." You and your husband should work together as a team, teaching your children what is acceptable and unacceptable behavior. Remember one day your children will grow up and leave, but your husband will still be your husband. Have proper priorities and relationships in your home and you'll avoid many breakdowns in your home life. How is your home a refuge for you, your husband, and your children?

_____

_____

_____

_____

_____

_____

_____

_____

_____

15. Explain your priority for time with your husband and children in relation to your job, church, and social life. There are many demands on a woman today when the added responsibility of earning income is listed with her daily chores. How does a Noble Woman balance her remaining time after work? Do you have enough time for all the areas of your life? What do you have the most trouble fitting in? How do you decide what takes priority if something has to be deleted from your schedule?

_____

_____

_____

_____

_____

_____

_____

_____

_____

16. What Biblical principles do you follow in raising your children or influencing other children in your life? Despite what has been said in the last decade about raising children, it's still the most important duty a woman has. (Not that a woman has to have children to be valuable in life.) A childless woman can influence another child. Some mothers have their hands very full with a houseful of children and no close relatives (and sometimes no husband) to help. These women would appreciate help from a childless friend in teaching their children the important things in life. According to the Bible, you should explain God's kingdom to children when they get up in the morning, as you travel here and there, as you sit down for meals, and when you put them to bed (Deuteronomy 6:7).

_____

_____

_____

_____

_____

_____

_____

_____

17. Humans have a unique mechanism for using time. They tend to expand an activity to fit the time available. In other words, if you list three activities for your day off, you'll take all day to finish those three. However, if you list six activities, you'll probably get all six done. Housework can be the biggest robber of time. You can always find more dirt to clean in a well-lived house. If you aren't careful to set time limits on certain chores, your spare time will be eaten away with cleaning. Homes that look like they belong on the pages of a magazine serve a purpose

different from homes that people "live in." Most husbands and children would prefer mom spend less time cleaning and more time with them. How many hours do you spend at home? What activities comprise the majority of those hours? Allow time for household chores, your children, cooking, relaxation, working at home, and hobbies. Do you ever combine activities at home? How? Do you know how much time different household chores take to accomplish?

_____

_____

_____

_____

_____

_____

_____

_____

_____

18. Describe the importance you attach to household and child-rearing chores. There are scores of books out today on how to keep a well-run household. Practically every woman's magazine runs tips on cleaning faster and better, organization, and quick recipes. Take advantage of the available information while adapting tips to fit your individual family home style. Be open to change and willing to drop ideas that no longer work for your family. There are also many helpful books and magazines, especially Christian oriented ones, about raising children, too. There are many aspects to raising children other than meeting their physical needs. Too much emphasis has been placed on physical needs (potty-training, learning to read, etc.) and not enough on teaching right and wrong (wisdom) and loving God (favor with God). Think of the four areas you've learned about. How do you meet your children's growing needs in each area?

_____

_____

_____

_____

_____

_____

_____

V-15

19. Describe family problems or relationships which have affected your life either positively or negatively. Was your childhood happy? Why? Why not? Do you usually get along well with siblings and parents? Has your relationship with any family member changed since childhood? Do you currently have any major conflicts with any of your relatives? Why are some members of your family, and not others, close? Which family member do you get along with best? Why? With which family member do you have the most conflicts? Why?

_____

_____

_____

_____

_____

_____

_____

_____

20. Is your perspective or relationship different with family members who are Christian as opposed to those who are non-Christian? Do you make any efforts to keep in contact with family members? Do you have a witness to non-Christian relatives? How do you encourage Christian relatives?

_____

_____

_____

_____

_____

_____

_____

_____

21. Neither spouse appreciates a partner who condemns his in-laws. You gain an added blessing from turning an in-law into a friend. Learn to accept counsel from the woman who raised your husband. Praise your husband to her, and you will gain her respect. Often a mother doesn't know how to let go of her son. If this is a problem with your mother-in-law, and you truly believe she is overstepping her limits, speak the truth in love. Love covers a multitude of sins and can cover any problems that may exist in this relationship. List any major conflicts you have with in-laws.

_____

_____

_____

_____

_____

_____

_____

_____

_____

22. Name any conflict between you and your husband regarding any of your in-laws. The devil will use this as a sore spot between you. As a Noble Woman, you can be an example of loving submission, and respectfully honor both sets of parents. Explain how you can better handle this source of conflict.

_____

_____

_____

_____

_____

_____

_____

_____

23. Explain why you think God placed certain relatives in your life. Nothing happens by accident. God has a plan for it all. He designed every intricate detail about you before you were born.

He has a purpose for every person in your life. Which relatives have profoundly affected you? What positive or negative effects have they worked in your life? Is there anything about your family you don't understand?

V-15

_____

_____

_____

_____

_____

_____

_____

_____

24. Allow God to take past hurts and expectations. Don't force yourself to forgive and forget; allow God to do the work through you. Holding back in this area can retard your ability to grow as a Noble Woman. Name one area or particular relationship you would like to improve upon within your family.

_____

_____

_____

_____

_____

_____

_____

_____

25. What is your relationship with your neighbors? When you read in the Bible you're to love your neighbors, do you take the term figuratively to mean all the people of the world and those you meet in the community? This is an accurate description of the general meaning, but you shouldn't forsake the literal meaning of loving those who live nearby. It's getting harder to know and love neighbors. Many neighborhoods are generally devoid of adults during daytime hours. Most people are caught up in their own busy lives and can't take the time to chat over the

backyard fence. Have you looked for ways to fulfill God's commandment to love your neighbors?

_____

_____

_____

_____

_____

_____

_____

_____

_____

26. What is your responsibility to the non-Christian world as a whole? How do you deal with that responsibility? What does the Bible have to say about dealing with the secular world? Your feelings toward the world at large tell you something about your commitment to God. Do you see the world as a place to minister, or a place to avoid contact? Do you look for opportunities to affect your world for God? Do you separate your concerns for this world from your Christian life? What do you think God has to say about this?

_____

_____

_____

_____

_____

_____

_____

_____

_____

27. Are there any areas of social contact you should improve? Even though Christians naturally place emphasis on the spiritual side of their nature, they're still basically social beings. Lack of social propriety can demean a Christian witness. You should be the example of good citizen, helpful neighbor, courteous customer, merciful driver, and understanding businessman. Do you assume these roles with a Christian attitude?

_____
_____
_____
_____
_____
_____
_____
_____
_____
_____

V-15

28. Do you have a relationship problem with anyone? Do you react well to and cooperate with family, friends, employers, managers, neighbors, church members and leaders, government officials and city workers? What about people you meet through school, while grocery shopping, or at social functions? A Noble Woman should be balanced enough to adapt to each of these social relationships. How can you build your strengths in these relationships?

_____
_____
_____
_____
_____
_____
_____
_____
_____

29. How do you keep your life organized? In your attempt to balance your growth, you should see a pattern emerge for organizing and coordinating all four areas. What organizational systems do you now use for your household, work, and ministry? What do you like or dislike in your system?

_____
_____
_____

_____
_____
_____
_____
_____
_____

30. To begin any kind of organizational system, you must have goals. Becoming a Noble Woman is a goal. The steps you take to become a Noble Woman are short-term goals. Think of the four areas of growth, and changes you are making in each area. These, too, are short-term goals. What are some short-term and long-term goals you have for your life? How do you plan to grow in wisdom, stature, and favor with God and men?

_____
_____
_____
_____
_____
_____
_____
_____
_____
_____
_____

SUMMARY

Growing socially, in favor with men, brings real radiance to the Noble Woman's life. The ability to get along well with others in any social situation is a blessing. For a Noble Woman to lovingly submit to her husband, train up her children in kindness, joyfully help her neighbors, enthusiastically work in church ministries, and encouragingly build her friendships is a sign of true Christianity. A Noble Woman needs to develop strong Christian relationships with her husband, family, and friends. Any fellowship problems need to be overcome with the love and compassion of Jesus. Do you have favor with men, especially fellow Christians? Be a peacemaker among men, the beloved of your husband, the friend that sticks closer than a brother, and you will be a Noble Woman.

ASSIGNMENT

Memorize Proverbs 3:25-28. Memorization should be easier after the past weeks of steady work. As you memorize these verses, pay attention to those that mention doing good to your neighbor.

Suggestion: I Peter 3:15 says you should always be ready with an answer when asked about God. What better answer could you give someone than quoting Scripture? Think of questions someone might ask you and how you can use your memorized verses to answer them. This is the way to really put memorization to good use.

V-15

Growing in Favor in Your Local Church

V-16

PURPOSE

To discover your role in the local church and the proper development of relationships in the Church. To determine the purposes of local churches.

OVERVIEW

". . . And have taught you publicly, and from house to house" (Acts 20:20 KJV). Here Paul mentions the system used by the disciples and members of the early Church (Acts 2) in bridging the gap between practicing Jews, who followed Jesus as the Messiah, and new, Gentile Christians who didn't attend the temple. The early Church established an identity separate from the Jewish temple. Its framework for working in God's kingdom became the basis for the local church. Having a clear image of why your local church exists, why you should go, and what you should do there, will help you grow in favor with men and become a Noble Woman. A local church exists for ministry. There you minister to God through worship, and God ministers to you through the preaching and teaching. The church is also a social organism whereby Christians minister to each other, and to non-Christians. The workings of the local church, and the Body of Christ (the Church as a whole), are intricate and rather profound. The Christian must understand those workings to properly perform his role in the Church.

DISCUSSION

Why do we have church buildings? Does the number of church meetings and services you attend determine your spirituality? Why do churches have more than one worship service weekly? Should you feel obligated to be involved in a church ministry? These are questions you should ask yourself as you learn how the local church fits into your social area of growth.

Purposes of the Church:

1. The Church, as a whole, is the spiritual Zion for this world. In I Peter 2, Peter addresses various Gentile Christians scattered in different cities. He groups them together as one Church in his words of encouragement to all Christians. Believers in Christ have a separate identity from the rest of the world. The local church provides a meeting place for each member of the Body of believers. Peter discusses this identity in verse 9, *"But you are a*

chosen people, a royal priesthood, a holy nation, a people belonging to God, that you may declare the praises of him who called you out of darkness into his wonderful light." Zion is the name God gives to his people in this world. In Psalm 87:6 He says your name is written in heaven as being from the nation of Zion. Zion grew from Abraham (Genesis 18:18). With the birth of Jesus, that blessing extended to all nations who accepted Jesus Christ as Savior. Then, believers became the Body of Christ, a spiritual Zion (Ephesians 2:17-18). *"For we were all baptized by one Spirit into one body — whether Jews or Greeks, slave or free — and we were all given the one Spirit to drink. Now the body is not made up of one part but of many"* (I Corinthians 12:13-14).

You shouldn't cut yourself off from the rest of the body by not attending church services on a regular basis. You should make every effort to unify with a group of Bible believing Christians (Ephesians 4:3). God's desire is for Christians to continually meet and fulfill His will in agreement and harmony. The local church building provides the place and opportunity for you to meet. There you can minister to God in worship, to each other in ministry, and to the world in outreach. The church provides a steady opportunity for preaching, teaching, missionary work, prophecy, and evangelism so all may grow together as one spiritual being. *"Prepare God's people for works of service, so that the body of Christ may be built up until we all reach unity in the faith and in the knowledge of the Son of God and become mature, attaining to the whole measure of the fullness of Christ"* (Ephesians 4:12-13).

2. The local body of believers should be a vehicle of blessing to those in the Church and community. In this day and age people automatically assume a government agency will help when someone is in trouble or need of advice. This present day policy usurps the responsibility of the Church. The local body of believers should have a storehouse of money and goods (derived from the tithes of the people) to meet the needs of its members and the community. The church, not the government, should give weekly groceries to families who can't make ends meet, clothing to needy children, and money to families with unemployed members (Acts 20:35, Revelation 2:19). The early Church simplified this business. Everyone brought all his money and valuables to the Church to share equally (according to need). Members often took their meals together; Paul admonished them to be sure all received equal portions of food. But the Church can bless in other ways as well. *"Is any one of you sick? He should call the elders of the church to pray over him and anoint him with oil in the name of the Lord. And the prayer offered in faith will make the sick person well"* (James 5:14-15). The records of the early Church, in the Book of Acts, name several occasions when the sick and disabled were healed by the laying on of hands and the prayers of the Church.

The Church is to bless its members by protecting them from evil deceptions and keeping them pure (Genesis 22:17, Ephesians 4:12). *"Guard yourselves and all the flock of which the Holy Spirit has made you overseers"* (Acts 20:28). Christians receive the blessing of the Holy Spirit and the gift of power through the prayers of the elders of the Church (Acts 8:17). As you receive blessings from your local church, joy wells up within your spirit. This great joy in serving the Lord is difficult to attain when cut off from the local church. *"Let us therefore make every effort to do what leads to peace and to mutual edification"* (Romans 14:19).

V-16

3. The church is an excellent training ground where Christians learn the workings of the Kingdom of Heaven. It's a place to learn how to operate in authority over a ministry or group of people. It's a revelation about how well you submit to authority; it proves whether or not you have a servant's heart. It teaches how to be last, that one day you may be first. The church system makes you comfortable with your future existence in the Kingdom of Heaven. One day you'll rule and reign with God (Revelation 2:26-27). In the church you can fulfill His commission to subdue the earth (Genesis 1:28) and gain spiritual power (I Corinthians 4:20). *"Blessed and holy are those who have part in the first resurrection. The second death has no power over them, but they will be priests of God and of Christ and will reign with him for a thousand years"* (Revelation 20:6).

The Church also teaches Christians about the Kingdom of God so they'll understand how to rule and reign with Him. Jesus began this by teaching His disciples the meaning of the parables He taught the world. He explained God's plan and the disciples' part in His plan. Each parable He taught explored, in some fashion, the workings of the Kingdom of God. Even today, the Holy Spirit constantly reveals more to the Church about His Kingdom. Certain activities are to be accomplished by the Church. Each local body has a particular message and ministry to its community (Revelation 2 and 3). Activities of the Church include:

a. preaching the Kingdom of Heaven is near.

b. telling the good news of Jesus Christ.

c. preaching the fulfillment of Old Testament prophecy in Jesus.

d. sending missionaries to tell all nations about Jesus.

e. baptizing in the name of Jesus Christ.

f. teaching people how to obey what Jesus commanded (not just teaching His commandments, but how to obey them).

g. being witnesses to the world.

4. The Church is an incubator for the growth of fellowship among Christians. You can't survive as a Christian without encouraging Christian friendships born out of the local church. The Church is a breeding ground for great Christian friendships where true brotherly love can spring up and unite people in an eternal bond. You just can't have the same kind of friendship with a non-Christian. *"Or what fellowship can light have with darkness? . . . What does a believer have in common with an unbeliever?"* (II Corinthians 6:14-15) Rather, you're to spend your time with other believers encouraging each other in the faith. (I Thessalonians 5:11) You should give to each other (Luke 6:38), have communion together (Luke 22:19) and fellowship on the Lord. *"From him the whole body, joined and held together by every supporting ligament, grows and builds itself up in love, as each part does its work"* (Ephesians 4:16).

Fellowship is the tie that binds the Church together. Those who break the bonds of fellowship by neglecting to attend services, judging fellow Christians, or merely sitting in the pews, damage their efforts to do the will of God. God said the world will know Christians by their love for each other. A Noble Woman will develop that bond of closeness with the members of her church. The first Church meetings after the day of Pentecost were conducted with a great joy and energy of spirit. Churches today should follow the example found in Acts 2:42-47, *"They devoted themselves to the apostles' teaching and to the fellowship, to the breaking of bread and to prayer. Everyone was filled with awe, and many wonders and miraculous signs were done by the apostles. All the believers were together and had everything in common. Selling their posessions and goods, they gave to anyone as he had need. Everyday they continued to meet together in the temple courts. They broke bread in their homes and ate together with glad and sincere hearts, praising God and enjoying the favor of all the people. And the Lord added to their number daily those who were being saved."*

5. The local church is the backbone for ministry to Christians within the Church and for ministry to non-Christians outside the Church. What place does a woman have in the actual workings of a church? Should the female half of the congregation participate in teaching, training, praying, praising, prophesying, encouraging, helping, counseling, and meeting needs of groups within the church? Look at the important role some women played in the Old Testament church and the crucial role of other women in the New Testament church to find the answer.

The Role of Women in the Old Testament:

1. **Eve.** Although Eve, the first woman, made the mistake first in the garden of Eden, God bestowed a great blessing on women through her. When Eve was created out of man it was as an equal partner. God expected her to subdue the earth along with Adam (Genesis 1:28). When Eve fell for the temptation of Satan, Adam didn't interfere in her free choice (Genesis 3:6). In Genesis 3:15 God gave Eve the promise of the Savior being born of a woman. God's forgiveness was so great He gave Eve the privilege of bringing redemption into the world. In all God's dealings with Adam and Eve, there's never any indication he treated Eve differently than Adam. Therefore, there's no reason to exclude women from participation in a worship service or communicating to God through prayer, prophecy, or singing.

2. **Sarah.** God's system of doing things is motivated by the policy that He can choose to bless whomever He wishes and choose whomever He wills to be a leader. *"I will have mercy on whom I have mercy, and I will have compassion on whom I have compassion"* (Exodus 33:19). He chose to have mercy on Sarah and allow her to bear the child of promise. God chose Sarah because of her barrenness; He works best through weakness. God can do some of His greatest works through weak women. Peter discusses the responsibility of wives and husbands in I Peter 3:1-7. He refers to Sarah as being the example of a beautiful woman. Her beauty came from the inner peace of submitting to her husband. Peter says *"You are her daughters if you do what is right and do not give way to fear."* You should do anything in God's house your

husband agrees is right for you to do. Peter also informs husbands to be sure to treat their wives as partners and heirs with the respect their positions require.

3. **Rachel and Leah.** These women, between the two of them, bore twelve sons who became the twelve tribes of Israel, an entire nation of people. God listened to Rachel and Leah when they called out to Him in prayer. Despite the natural conflicts that came from being sisters married to the same man, these women raised twelve sons to be strong leaders. Rachel's son, Joseph, became not only a leader of his own nation, but second only to Pharoah in leading the Egyptians. His mother's teaching surely helped him never to doubt God in times of serious trouble.

4. **Deborah.** The Book of Judges depicts a time of sin, servitude, repentance, and salvation for Israel. This four-step process was repeated twelve times over the years. Each time the Israelites pleaded with God to help them escape their bondage to a foreign power and repented of their sins of idolatry, God answered them with a godly leader who would bring victory and peace to their lives. Deborah was one of those people. Though married, it was Deborah, not her husband, who ruled Israel. She settled disputes among the people the way Moses did. She directed the captain of her army, and received direction from God concerning her people. God didn't hesitate to use her in the position of leader. God also used another woman to deliver the Israelites from the enemy.

5. **Esther.** Esther was also a leader of her people. God enabled her to marry the king who was keeping Jews in captivity. Esther was generally submissive to her husband, the king. When her people were in danger of being annihilated, she boldly forsook the law that required her to be summoned before appearing before the king. Using her sweet charms, she revealed that her people were in danger from one of his laws. Because of her previous submission to him, the king didn't punish her for speaking, but instead saved her people from the fatal law. Esther was put in a high position to accomplish the salvation of the Jewish race. God will use a woman in any position if her nature will accomplish His goals better than a man's.

The Role of Women in the New Testament Church:

1. **Phoebe.** Phoebe was Paul's co-worker, and probably the person who delivered his letter to the church in Rome. They were told to receive her as Paul's equal and assist her in her work there for God. In the last chapter of Romans Paul mentions nine women and their work in the church. That they obviously held important positions shows women can be appointed to any position in the Church.

2. **Chloe.** Chloe is mentioned in I Corinthians. Under her direction Paul was informed of the unspiritual behavior of the Corinthian church. The verse refers to Chloe's household. Either she was without a husband, and therefore, the head of her house, or she was a Christian and her husband wasn't. In any case, Paul respected her authority.

3. **Mary.** There were several Marys in the New Testament

Church who had important positions, but Martha and Lazarus' sister, Mary, held a special place in Jesus' eyes. Their house in Bethany was the closest place Jesus ever had to a home. While Martha busied herself preparing meals, Mary sat at Jesus' feet and listened. This position, sitting at the feet of a teacher, was traditionally a man's place of learning. Martha was shocked at Mary's "manly" behavior, but Jesus recognized it as the better place to be at the time. Jesus thus identified the role of a student as being for men and women in God's Kingdom.

4. **Euodia and Syntyche.** These women were members of the church in Philippi and probably held services in their homes as well. Their work was known to Paul. He gave them counsel to settle their differences, as he often did to the male leaders of the Church. They are thought to have been deaconesses.

5. **The elect lady.** The disciple John wrote one of his letters to this unnamed woman. It's difficult to tell if this was a personal letter or one written to the pastor (a woman) of a small church. In any event, the letter is written along the lines of those written to other churches. Special mention is made of loving each other in Christ (a common commandment to the early churches) and of being very careful to know if someone has come in Jesus' name to preach or teach. Some early churches were being taught erroneous doctrine by deceptive people who weren't Christians. John warns this woman about the same danger and instructs her not to let any of these people into her home.

A Note of Caution: Although there are numerous references to women being a vital part of the church, a word must be said about the verses in I Timothy 2:11-14 which refer to keeping women silent in the church and not permitting them to teach. Taken in context, this passage is meant for a specific situation. This particular church had a problem with headship and women usurping authority. The women didn't understand their husbands were to be their head and umbrella of protection. Women should always have the permission of husband and pastor before proceeding with a position in the Church. This isn't an unusual request. In later verses Paul states that men also have to be approved by the pastor before working in the Church. A Noble Woman always works with her husband's blessing. Once a woman receives the proper authority, she's free to assume any role in the Church as an equal laborer for God.

SUMMARY

It takes more than one service a week to accomplish the goals of the local church in God's eyes. Everyone must do his part to encourage unity in the church. You must be involved with church ministries to be a vehicle of blessing to others. You must assume positions of leadership and be willing to be trained and taught in preparation for the future Kingdom of Heaven. Attend a local church regularly and often to ensure you're ministering to God, fellow Christians, and the community. Be willing to cultivate friendships in the church and fellowship with the believers in local congregations. As a Noble Woman, you must be an example of the role of women in the church. Assume responsibility, with your husband's and pastor's blessing, to do the work God has called you to do. *"And let us consider how we may spur one another on toward love and good deeds. Let us not give up meeting together, as some are in the habit of doing, but let us encourage one another — and all the more as you see the Day approaching"* (Hebrews 10:24-25).

V-16

ASSIGNMENT

Memorize Proverbs 3:29-30. Your neighbor includes those who live by you and those who sit by you in church.

Suggestion: Keep all 3 x 5 cards with memory verses from the same chapter in order. Using them as flash cards, quickly go from one to the next to help you piece each week's memorization into one flowing recitation.

TABLE 7

PARABLES THAT TEACH ABOUT THE KINGDOM OF GOD

The Parable of the:	Found in:
Sower	Matthew
Weeds	Matthew
Mustard Seed	Matthew
Yeast	Matthew
Hidden Treasure	Matthew
Pearl	Matthew
Net	Matthew
Child	Matthew
Lost Sheep	Matthew
Unmerciful Servant	Matthew
Workers in the Vineyard	Matthew
Two Sons	Matthew
Tenants	Matthew
Wedding Banquet	Matthew
Ten Virgins	Matthew
Talents	Matthew
Sheep and Goats	Matthew
Growing Seed	Mark
Lamp on a Stand	Mark
Rich Fool	Luke
Narrow Door	Luke
Lost Coin	Luke
Shrewd Manager	Luke
Pharisee and the Tax Collector	Luke
Shepherd and His Flock	John
Vine and the Branches	John

Lesson 17
Growing in Favor with Husband and Children

V-17

PURPOSE

To learn how to grow in favor with your husband and how to raise children up to call you blessed.

OVERVIEW

It's almost derogatory these days for a woman to refer to herself primarily as a wife and mother. Though the two duties aren't comparable, they're interwoven in the delicate fabric of family life. The importance of family life in your heart is determined by the strength in which you weave your roles of wife and mother.

Women shouldn't have to apologize for wanting to nurture their families as a primary goal in life. It's their God-given right to devote their time and efforts to making the home a pleasurable place to be. As God calls you to be a Noble Woman, He also calls you to be a noble wife and mother. Many sincere Christian women have gone off base in their attitudes and ways of ministering to husband and children. Regard those roles as the ministry they are. Serve your family in quiet humility to help draw them closer to Jesus. What does Scripture tell us about the live-giving roles of wife and mother? By examining what Scripture has to say about these two duties, memorizing God's Word on the subject, and trusting God to enable you to walk after His pattern, you will begin your life as a noble wife and mother.

DISCUSSION

Being a Noble Wife:

One of the hardest lessons for a Christian woman to learn is that of the submissive wife (Ephesians 5:22, Colossians 3:18, I Peter 3:1). Since the curse in the Garden of Eden, women's natures have been in strife with their husbands'. Their desire is to rule their husbands instead of following the Godly principle of submission. Added to the natural inclination to rebel against a husband's headship is the firmly planted idea that submission is outdated, cruel, chauvenistic, unintelligent, and unrealistic. This atheistic and humanistic way of thinking misses God's point. *"For the husband is the head of the wife as Christ is the head of the church, his body, of which he is the Savior. Now as the church submits to Christ, so also wives should submit to their husbands in everything"* (Ephesians 5:23-24).

God does everything in an orderly fashion. He has a plan, and knows what's best. In every institution there must be one person who makes the final decision. On a board of directors there's always a chairman who can break a tie vote. There must be an ultimate authority, even in the home, otherwise home life becomes a dichotomy created by two decision-making powers not always headed toward the same goal. Conflicts arise. Divorce is often inevitable. In marriage, God arranged for the husband to be the final authority. The wife, when performing her role correctly, offers her ideas, opinions, and feelings on a matter for her husband's consideration. With the responsibility of making the final choice no longer hers, she has a better perspective of the situation and can guide her husband to a decision without fear of failure. The husband can then appreciate input from a different perspective and can make a better decision.

If the wife continues to offer her views and agrees to her husband's indisputable authority, and if the husband continues to lovingly listen to his wife's input in making timely decisions, then the marriage will succeed and be a living testimony to the glory of God. As an extra component for victory, the husband who looks to the Lord will create an unbroken bond against any antimarriage force. *"Though one may be overpowered, two can defend themselves. A cord of three strands is not quickly broken"* (Ecclesiastes 4:12). The cord of husband, wife, and Holy Spirit stands strong against unhappiness or divorce.

How does a wife submit to her husband? In what ways can she offer her views? What qualities does a noble wife need to have to be a submissive wife?

First, wives cannot follow blindly after husbands, agreeing in ignorance with what they say and do. Nehemiah 10:28-29 makes it clear that wives must understand the decisions, good or bad, their husbands make. If a husband decides to obey God in a matter, the wife must make the decision to obey God for herself. Though protected from Satan's tricks by her husband's leadership, a wife is responsible for her own walk with the Lord. When overseers and deacons were appointed in I Timothy 3, not only was the husband's record under scrutiny, but also the wife's trustworthiness.

What does a wife do if she's a Christain but her husband isn't? Does that keep her from becoming a noble wife? Certainly not. I Corinthians 7 addresses this issue and explains that though the wife shouldn't leave her husband (verse 10), she's free if he leaves her (verse 15). More importantly the husband of a believing wife has a special sanction in God's eyes (verses 14, 16, 17). Her submission to him can also win him over to the Lord (I Peter 3:1).

The story of Abigail, Nabal, and David found in I Samuel 25 is an excellent example of what it means to be a noble wife.

It was a custom at that time that small bands of armies (David's

126

being one of them) would go in to the hills to perfect their skills. When the flocks of wealthy city dwellers were driven into the hills, the small armies policed the area, protecting flocks and shepherds from thieves in exchange for food. In addition, they were invited, along with the neighbors, to enjoy the seasonal sheep shearing festivities. This was David's situation. David asked Nabal for his due because his men had guarded Nabal's property so well. Nabal's response was inappropriate. Even if he didn't realize the valuable service David's men provided, he was being asked in goodwill to allow a group of trustworthy men (proven by the testimony of Nabal's own men) to enjoy the bounty of his wealth. There were undoubtedly many people partaking of Nabal's generosity during that time. David's men had already proven they meant no harm; they were only in need of food.

V-17

Nabal responded true to his surly and mean character. He answered David's protection of his flocks with a slur. *"Many servants are breaking away from their masters these days"* (verse 10). He was trying to upset David with a remark about David's relationship with King Saul from whom he was fleeing. This remark was untrue, but did it damage. David rallied his men to ride up to Nabal's house and slaughter all the men.

Enter Nabal's wife Abigail. The first thing the Bible says about her is that she was intelligent and beautiful. Everything Scripture tells about Abigail after this is seen in that light. As soon as Abigail hears of the mess her husband made she was quick to act. She set a plan into action to save her household. Never did she openly or spitefully criticize her husband. Scripture reveals she was probably accustomed to handling the affairs of the household without her husband's help. She might have had experience in trying to cover up his mistakes. She was comfortable moving among men and speaking her ideas, and commanding servants.

Abigail could have used several opportunities to get even with her husband. She didn't hunt him down to berate him for his foolish behavior. She overlooked his creating trouble. Instead she got busy to right the wrong. While she got ready to leave, Abigail had a chance to "let Nabal have a piece of her mind." She didn't do this either. It appears she avoided aggravating Nabal. When discussing the circumstance with David, she kept her dignity while humbly asking for mercy. She didn't elaborate on the injustice of her life. She didn't say more than was necessary. Later she again had the perfect opportunity to take out all her frustration on her husband when he was drunk. She could have broken the news of her visit to David when Nabal was in a good mood from his party. Instead she waited until he was sober.

Abigail knew two of the best defenses for a wife—silence and timing. She knew when to be quiet and go about her work, and when to speak (to David and to Nabal). She showed concern for her husband and his property even though he was a foolish man. She didn't desert him; she helped him all she could, in spite of himself. She used her intellect to counteract her husband's foolishness and to win favor with David.

God honored Abigail's sense of selfless duty to her husband. She didn't try to rid herself of her unfit husband (she could have let David kill him). Because of that, God himself struck Nabal with a heart attack that quickly killed him, freeing Abigail to be married to another. God knew Abigail deserved a better husband; one who wouldn't have holes in his umbrella of protection; one who would one day be king.

God doesn't promise every wife who has a foolish man for a husband that if she's faithful to him, she'll one day marry a king; but He does promise to take care of her.

There are behavior patterns that characterize a submissive wife. Develop these traits and you'll find it easy to be submissive.

1. Give your husband what he desires. (I Corinthians 7:34)

2. Respect him. (Ephesians 5:33)

3. Be kind to him. (Titus 2:5)

4. Let him have final say. (Numbers 30:10-15)

5. Tell your husband about your spiritual walk. (Judges 13:10)

6. Build your home with wisdom. (Proverbs 14:1)

7. Serve meals with love. (Proverbs 15:17)

8. Provide an atmosphere of peace and quiet. (Proverbs 17:1)

9. Don't start quarrels. This must be an important word of advice; look at how many times it's mentioned. (Proverbs 17:14; 19:13; 21:9; 21:19; 25:24; 27:15)

10. Be kind hearted. (Proverbs 11:17)

11. Be prudent. (Proverbs 19:14)

12. Don't be ill-tempered. (Proverbs 21:19)

13. Develop wisdom, understanding, and knowledge in running your household. (Proverbs 24:3)

14. Be a Noble Woman. (Proverbs 31:10)

15. Be patient. (I Corinthians 13:4)

16. Don't boast. (I Corinthians 13:4)

17. Don't be rude. (I Corinthians 13:5)

18. Don't be easily angered. (I Corinthians 13:5)

19. Don't keep track of your husband's wrongs. (I Corinthians 13:5)

20. Protect, trust, hope for, and persevere with your husband. (I Corinthians 13:7)

21. Don't be childish in dealing with your husband. (I Corinthians 13:11)

As your marriage progresses through the honeymoon, disillusionment, resolution, acceptance, and blessing stages, remember your marriage vows. You committed yourself to your husband for better or worse, and unless he walks out on you, you have no right to separate yourself from him. Divorce is a "fire escape" in today's marriages. If you had no chance to escape a fire, you'd be committed to staying and putting out the flames. Don't consider divorce an option; learn to stay together and put out the flames. Be willing to do whatever it takes to stay together. Christians have eternal hope that God gives absolute justice in the end for whatever they may have to endure. The Holy Spirit can change a husband's heart when given time to work.

V-17

A Noble Mother:

Being a mother is hard work. Raising children from birth to adulthood is no easy matter. From the day he's born you must learn to meet a child's every need while allowing him to gain independence little by little. To meet a child's needs, pay attention to the four areas of growth. As you grow in wisdom, stature, and favor with men and God, so do your children.

Be sure and tell them the things of God to help them grow in wisdom. *"Impress them on your children. Talk about them when you sit at home and when you walk along the road, when you lie down and when you get up"* (Deuteronomy 6:7). Allow them to make small decisions early in life. Show them the difference between right and wrong, and how to choose right.

It's easy to meet the physical needs of a child. Mothers tend to overemphazise the details of this area of growth and neglect the others. Provide food from the four food groups (meat, fruit and vegetables, dairy, grains and cereal) when they are hungry, sleep when they're tired, regular baths, and medical treatment when they're sick. Throw in doses of sunshine and opportunities for physical play and and your child will have no difficulty in growing physically to peak performance.

It isn't the Sunday School teacher's job to train your children spiritually; it's yours. *"Teach (the words of God) to your children"* (Deuteronomy 11:19). Help your children be spiritual beings from an early age (Mark 10:13).

What to teach your children about God:

1. God's plan of salvation
2. God's plan for them as individuals
3. How to grow in wisdom, stature, and favor with God and men
4. How to pray
5. How to find direction from the Holy Spirit
6. How to worship God
7. How to be a witness
8. How to find their special purpose in life
9. How God's Word is true
10. How to develop a relationship with God
11. How to find answers in the Bible
12. How to build faith
13. How to learn from God and others
14. How to accept discipline from God and parents
15. How to accept themselves in God's eyes
16. How much God loves them
17. How much they should love others

18. How to be a good friend

19. How to react to sin

20. To memorize Scripture

21. To live according to Biblical principles

22. To have peace, joy, patience, kindness, love, goodness, faithfulness, gentleness, and self-control

One of the hard lessons in life for young children is growing socially. Mothers can give their children a valuable advantage in life by teaching them how to get along well with others. It goes against a child's nature to share or take turns. (Adults who socialize poorly are called "childish.") Help children, through prayer and patient direction, overcome selfish behavior. Be a good example. Parents who aren't willing to share a favorite chair, have trouble giving up control of the TV, or can't help a neighbor in need, are poor examples.

Having children gives you an excellent opportunity to make up for the lessons you didn't learn early enough in life. Realize, however, that God didn't give you children to live out *your* dreams. They must fulfill *their own* dreams. You can teach them things you wish you'd known at their age; but you must allow them to make their own mistakes. Raising children is the gradual process of letting go. Think of yourself as letting go of your child's hand a little each day until he's walking entirely on his own. God will help you accomplish this if you trust His Word about raising children.

"He who spares the rod hates his son, but he who loves him is careful to discipline him" (Proverb 13:24). Both parents share the responsibility of disciplining children. *"Discipline your son, for in that there is hope; do not be a willing party to his death"* (Proverb 19:18). He will be rebellious as an adult if he isn't disciplined as a child. You need to provide an inheritance of character in your child's life (Proverb 17:6).

The reason for disciplining is simple. Children grow up with a selfish nature (Proverb 20:11). They're sinners "in the raw," so to speak. Children do whatever they want until someone tells them to stop. Once someone tells them "No, that's not allowed," they've learned a boundary. Small children continue to go places they shouldn't and do things which are wrong. They do this to learn where their limitations are. It's a scary feeling to think there are no limits in your life. Instead of freedom comes insecurity. Children seek their limits so they can relax and explore the world within the boundaries their parents set; but once the limits are established, they are adept at testing them to see if the boundaries are true. In other words, they continue to do what you've told them not to in order to see if you'll discipline each time they disobey. This sets a true boundary. Eventually the true boundaries are accepted without challenge (except for periodic testing). Many parents' downfall has been not to stay true to boundaries. A parent must be consistent in rule-setting and discipline in order to be effective. Teaching children that you will spank if they jump on the bed one time, and only scream at them another leaves confusing guidelines for them to follow. Throughout childhood then your children will break your rules, taking the risk that this will be the day you don't spank.

A wise mother doesn't fluctuate. Honor your word at all times (don't make idle promises to children) and they'll know you mean what you say. Suit the discipline to the offense, and keep it the same each time. Husbands and wives must be supportive of each other and discipline similarly. When a child learns he can play one parent against the other, there will be trouble in the home for years to come. One parent shouldn't be the "heavy," either. Discipline should be swift, immediate, and consistent, dealt out by either parent.

Balance discipline with mercy as your Heavenly Father does. If your child disobeys because of strong temptation and is truly repentant, you might lighten the correction to build trust. You want your child to know he can trust you to discipline fairly. You want him to feel your trust in him so he'll reveal the truth to you about his behavior. Establishing this pattern early saves many heartaches in the teen-age years.

Don't spank out of anger; spank out of love. This is easier said than done, and appears a contradiction in terms. Don't fail to shower your children with love as you correct their wrongs. When you show anger at a child for perhaps ruining your possessions, or frustration over a repeated offense, or resentment at having to take time to discipline, you risk the danger of your child assuming you're rejecting *him,* as opposed to rejecting his wrong *action.* Be encouraging about future behavior after correcting a present wrong doing.

"Take to heart all the words I have solemnly declared to your this day, so that you may command your children to obey carefully all the words of this law." (Deuteronomy 32:46). Give good gifts to your children (Matthew 7:11). Impart to them the Holy Spirit (Acts 2:39). Don't exasperate them (Ephesians 6:4). This happens when a parent is too critical of a child's behavior and hasn't differentiated between actual rebellion and mere childish behavior. Childish behavior shouldn't be punished, after all *child*-ish is what they are. Don't expect children to be adults. *"When I was a child, I thought as a child, I spake as a child"* (I Corinthians 13:11). Children shouldn't be punished for asking incessant questions, being fidgety, making bad decisions, forgetting, or being emotional. This is normal. Allow them to portray childish qualities (up to the point of infringing on another's rights) while gently instructing them about better behavior.

Tell your children about the work of God in your local church. *"Has anything like this ever happened in your days or in the days of your forefathers? Tell it to your children, and let your children tell it to their children, and their children to the next generation"* (Joel 1:2-3). Give them a good perspective of the role of the Church in their lives by praising, never condemning, the Church and its leaders. Help them be spiritually aware by controlling the outside influences of television and radio in the home. Arrange an atmosphere of peace for your family to come home to and take refuge in.

V-17

Mothers are to love their children, be self-controlled and not given to anger in discipline. Be busy with the care of the children — don't slight their growth in any area. Be kind. Provide a home that is fun to play in and invite friends to, but above all, put your husband's needs above those of the children so your children may gain the security that comes from having a mother and father committed to each other for life (Titus 2:4-5).

SUMMARY

Being a Noble Woman gives you a head start on being a noble wife. "*A wife of noble character is her husband's crown*" (Proverb 12:4). If a wife's desire is to please her husband (I Corinthians 7:34) and she looks to God to show her how, she will cause his love for her to grow. Accept your position of submissive wife with dignity and pleasure, know the responsibility for the family is off your shoulders. Be full of encouraging ideas for your husband and give him support in the decision-making he must assume. Follow the pattern of Abigail, who was intelligent, beautiful, and helpful, though married to a foolish man. You can't go wrong by filling your home with love. If you've chosen to put your family above your own desires or accomplishments in life, congratulate yourself on fulfilling God's desire for you. You're a Noble Woman.

Adding to the demanding requirements of a noble wife are the God-given duties of raising children and being a noble mother. Forget about perfection in the household. Strive for a place of joy in which to live. Teach your children to follow in your steps of growing in wisdom, stature, and favor with God and men. Raise your children according to Scripture, giving support to your husband in discipline. Your children will arise and call you blessed (Proverb 31:28).

ASSIGNMENT

Memorize Proverb 3:31-32. This verse is especially helpful to wives and mothers. We must rise above any violence and strife around us to maintain an atmosphere of peace in our hearts as an example in our homes.

Suggestion: "*The word of God is living and active. Sharper than any double-edged sword, it penetrates even to dividing soul and spirit, joints and marrow; it judges the thoughts and attitudes of the heart*" (Hebrews 4:12). Is your attitude right toward God concerning your memory work? Confess any misgivings you might have about memorizing God's Word. Treat the words you are memorizing as the life-building force they are.

Lesson 18
What's a Housewife to Do?

V-18

PURPOSE

To understand Biblical principles for building a home. To learn how to be the creative, unifying force in your family's life.

OVERVIEW

The Noble Woman in Proverbs 31 had a busy life. She grew in wisdom, stature, and favor with God and men. She met her husband's needs and provided a loving home for her children; but if you examine the verses written about her, you'll notice a proportionally large amount of verses concern daily household tasks. Selecting wool and flax, preparing food, making lists of chores, sewing clothes, and making beds filled her days. It's the mundane chores of running a household and keeping it clean that identify a woman as caretaker of the family. Though anyone can do those duties, no one else can take her place in the home life.

The way a Noble Woman performs these tasks marks her family as one receiving the loving encouragement it needs to be all it can for God. This lesson will cover general principles to guide you in housekeeping and achieving the kind of home atmosphere pleasing to God.

Part of the practical side of building family life is being the unifying force in the home. A wife and mother bonds sibling to sibling, children to father, and all of them to her. The best way of building and maintaining this bond is to create quality moments in family life, benchmarks of tradition cherished by family members, and to be a constant source of endearing ideas for family enjoyment. Sometimes the creativity needed to keep a family alive is forgotten or absorbed by the energy used in the practicalities of housework, laundry, meal planning, etc. A list of 35 family ideas is provided at the end of the lesson to help you be a resource of life for your family.

DISCUSSION
Practicalities

There are many sources today that give quick efficient help in running your household well. Have you ever considered going to the Bible for information? God is concerned about every area of your daily life. He has provided living words of wisdom about housekeeping and family life in His Word.

1. **Organize.** The first step in approaching a smoothly run household is to find the appropriate organizational system for your needs and family style. Systems abound, but only one molds to your unique situation. Once you discover it, put it to use. *'This is what the Lord says: Put your house in order"* (II Kings 20:1). Putting a house in order is a lifelong task. Appropriate this Bible principle for your family.

2. **Delegate.** People who accomplish the most are those who have someone else do it. Delegating responsibility is a Biblical principle established by Moses. Read Exodus 18:13-26. This is a story of a man who has too much to do and too little time. Sometimes mothers are like that. They think the only ones who can properly make a bed are themselves. They believe they are the only ones who know how to sort laundry or put things away in the right place. Moses thought he, too, was the only one who could do his job properly. His father-in-law had to tell him to pick helpers to do part of the work. So it should be in your household. *"Have them serve . . . but have them bring every difficult case to you; the simple cases they can decide themselves"* (Exodus 18:22). Give simple jobs to other family members; don't be concerned if the finished product doesn't meet your personal standards. You're fighting a losing battle if you seek perfection. With practice and praise from you, they will get better and you'll have one less chore to do yourself. Consider the idea of having family members switch responsibilities periodically so all members know how to do the most common household tasks.

3. **Prioritize.** Have a method for dealing with priorities in your life. In addition to choosing and working out a system of management for the home, a housewife needs to have a way to balance her day according to priorities. The duties of a housewife can be divided among three headings — the important, the essential, and everything else. On your daily list of things to do, you should know which category each chore falls under. Label "A" for the important things you need to do, like having your devotions, training your children, or spending time with your husband. Label "B" those items that are essential, such as laundry, having a dentist appointment, or feeding your family. Everything else is a "C." Each day you should work the important around the essential. Do everything else in any time that is left. Use wisdom in distinquishing "B"s from "C"'s. Don't forget to put your "A's" on the list. Often the essentials try to crowd what is important in our lives. *" 'Everything is permissible' — but not everything is beneficial. 'Everything is permissible' — but not everything is constructive. Nobody should seek his own good, but the good of others"* (I Corinthians 10:23-24).

4. **Eliminate and concentrate.** These two words "pack a wallop" when it comes to household efficiency. It's the simplest plan for any situation. Eliminate weaknesses and concentrate on strengths. Eliminate surplus projects in your life and concentrate on talents. In the kitchen, eliminate gadgets and concentrate on using appliances to their fullest capacity. Eliminate daydreaming about what you want in a house, and concentrate on what you have. Eliminate duplicates of anything and concentrate on living a simple lifestyle. Too much clutter in a house invites confusion.

Confusion adds to double-mindedness that creates unstability (James 1:8). Your family breathes in the philosophy of life you breathe out.

V-18

5. **Put first things first.** *"But seek first his kingdom and his righteousness, and all these things will be given to you as well"* (Matthew 6:33). More than pertaining just to priorities, this verse contains wisdom about planning your day and training your children. If you attend to the important matters first, and teach your children to fulfill responsibilites first, you will reap a harvest of blessing from God for yourself and increased maturity for your children. Learn to delay satisfaction by accomplishing the difficult first. Develop this in your children.

6. **Keep things in perspective.** Women tend to view everything in their lives as connected to themselves; men tend to separate their lives into parts. Therefore if a woman thinks she's a lousy housekeeper, she'll think she's a lousy person altogether. In her mind, every fault reflects on everything else she does. This is a dangerous thought pattern that adds depression to your list of troubles. Don't fall into the trap of associating what you *do* with who you *are*. When your neat house prohibits your family from enjoying itself, you've lost your persepctive. If your husband criticized your last meal, think of the time he thanked you for ironing his shirt. Don't be afraid to delegate your work because someone else can do a job as well as or better than you. Making mistakes in your work doesn't exclude you from the noble wife and mother award. It's a fact of being a housewife that some things just don't get done on time, correctly, or at all. *"Trust in the Lord with all your heart and lean not on your own understanding"* (Proverbs 3:5).

7. **Know when you're too busy.** If you have no time to spend with God; if you catch yourself hurrying kids through the day to get it all done; or if you have to make an appointment to see your husband, you're too busy. God doesn't want your life to get out of your control. Family life takes a huge commitment of time (especially in the beginning stages) to work well. Each family member has to limit outside commitments. Be the example for your family members and help them not be overcommitted. When household responsibilites overwhelm you, read Psalm 46:10. *"Be still, and know that I am God."* If you don't have time for a certain activity, then it isn't time for that activity to be done. *"There is a time for everything, and a season for every activity under heaven"* (Ecclesiastes 3:1).

8. **Have a place for everything** and keep everything in its place. Although you studied the problem of being overly critical and at odds with your family in keeping a neat house, your family should understand the need to have a place for items regularly used, to eliminate bickering or hunting for misplaced items. Again, you must be the example. Have a regular place to store your keys and purse, keep drawers neat. Put family-used items (such as scissors and tape) in a convenient location. Make everyone aware of the responsibility of replacing items (in the proper place) after using them. Any problems with this can be discussed during family meetings.

9. **Allow time for regular self-examination.** *"Test me, O Lord, and try me, examine my heart and my mind"* (Psalm 26:2). This is to help you make sure you're accomplishing all you think you ought, to evaluate methods used for organization and cleaning hints, and to check your priority system to see if the important things are being done. Check yourself against Scripture you've learned. Are you delegating and praising your family for helping, or are you gradually assuming their responsibilities again by doing jobs over for them? Have family meetings to inform members of changes in household rules, jobs, or organization methods. Keep family meetings of this type informal, short, and infrequent to gain your husband's support.

10. **Spend time with each family member.** When you think of being a housekeeper, you think of cleaning the house. This is only a portion, though a large portion, of housekeeping. While you may be delegating much of this responsibility to other family members, this doesn't give you time to be lazy. You must emphasize to your family that their help enables you to give time to other matters equally important in keeping a household a nice place to live. No matter how much cleaning you delegate, there will always be cleaning tasks left to do. The list can seem endless when you consider windows, baseboards, dirty walls, cabinets, the stove, oven, and refrigerator. You can be certain a family won't notice when you clean these things, only when you don't. Even these cleaning chores shouldn't consume too much of your time. Remember the story of Mary, Martha, and Jesus in the Bible? Martha scurried around doing the cleaning and cooking while Mary spent time with Jesus. Who did Jesus say spent her time wisely? Mary. Spend more time with your family and they won't care that you spend less time cleaning. This is excellent advice for company as well. Company is less impressed by fancy meals and a spotless home (and a harried hostess, as a result) than by a hostess who enjoys their presence.

11. **Don't waste time.** *"Have nothing to do with the fruitless deeds of darkness, but rather expose them. For it is shameful even to mention what the diosbedient do in secret. But everything exposed by the light becomes visible, for it is light that makes everything visible . . . Be very careful, then, how you live — not as unwise but as wise, making the most of every opportunity"* (Ephesians 5:11-16). Use your time wisely as a housekeeper. This becomes increasingly important as you assume responsibilites outside the home. This doesn't mean you must always fill your minutes with work, or spend all free time with your family. God created the Sabbath principle of rest to allow for fun and relaxation in your schedule. When it *is* time to work, cultivate the fruit of self-control to accomplish what God requires of you. Frittering away endless time is as much a sin as overwork. Both are a sign of no self-control.

12. **Preschoolers demand more of a mother's time than any other age.** A Noble Woman must account for this extra attention required from her. At a time when two-paycheck families are the norm, it's wise for the mother of young children to prayerfully consider the possibility of staying at home until children are in school. Pediatricians are more convinced than ever that the

majority of a child's character is developed by age 3. If you were convinced that spending three years in daily care would determine the success of your child's entire life, wouldn't you sacrifice to be there? *"And if anyone causes one of these little ones who believe in me to sin, it would be better for him to be thrown into the sea with a large millstone tied around his neck"* (Mark 9:42). The decision to work outside the home where there are preschoolers should be a matter of utmost prayer, seeking God's direction for your family. The Noble Woman's example in Proverbs 31 shows a favorable response from God. She conducted business outside the home, but she controlled her time by being her own boss. It doesn't say if she worked while the children were young, but remember, these verses refer to her whole lifetime. In any case, you're responsible for the way your children are being raised, even if you delegate the duty to someone else. In caring for children, it isn't the physical needs of care that are so important as the other areas of growth. Only a mother can give a mother's loving approval, encouragement, or security to her child.

V-18

13. **Older children need attention, too.** Once your children are school age, they need reinforcement of the basic values taught them as young children. This cannot be left to teachers. While the damaging effects of this world and the devil are strong, the wise mother can protect her children by bathing them in prayer when they aren't at home and providing a strong Christian atmosphere to encourage them when they are home. *"I have no greater joy than to hear that my children are walking in the truth"* (III John 4).

14. **Make "home" a special place.** Home life revolves around the nurturing role of the woman of the house. She's the designer who creates the atmosphere of home life. Make your home a desirous place to be. Provide encouragement, appreciation, and a refuge in times of trouble. Your home should be a place where each member feels special and is treated with tender, loving care. Each member should feel the trust of the others and be able to be honest about his feelings. The home should be the place where standards are set for members to carry with them when they leave home each day. *"Do not let any unwholesome talk come out of your mouths, but only what is helpful for building others up according to their needs, that it may benefit those who listen"* (Ephesians 4:29) Be sensitive to the needs of your family Is it time to study? Make the house quiet and comfortable, with study supplies on hand. Is it time for family fun? Fill your home with uplifting music, games, books, or television programs. Take the initiative to find family activities everyone enjoys. Is your family hungry? Serve a meal with pleasure and thankfulness. Has it been awhile since your family has talked together? Arrange a peaceful evening at home. Planning ahead and setting the atmosphere for your family's needs incubates a lifelong love for the home in each family member. You could leave your children no greater inheritance and provide your husband with no greater support than to provide the proper atmosphere in the home.

15. **Be hospitable.** While maintaining a happy home life for your family, keep in mind the directive of Jesus to care for others. It's

a great gift to give a home to someone in need. *"Offer hospitality to one another without grumbling"* (I Peter 4:9). Jesus always opened His life to those in need. You mustn't be selfish with the blessing God has given you in having a home. It's a great witness to your children and the world when you give up your privacy and open your precious home to others. *"Do not forget to entertain strangers, for by so doing some people have entertained angels without knowing it"* (Hebrews 13:2). Being hospitable means sharing the benefits of home life with the friendless and fatherless. It means celebrating with friends who cannot return the favor, or with families younger than yours who can use your example. Above all, it means opening your door to the non-Christian so he might better see Jesus. There is no better witness for Jesus than seeing an actual Christian family living everyday life.

16. **Help center your family's attention on Jesus** and the Bible's focus on the importance of family. A strong sense of family identity is what bonds each family member to the others. The little family traditions you have mark your family as unique in God's kingdom. The family looks to the mother to provide pleasant memories as the background for family living. Here is a list of 35 ideas to help creativity blossom within your heart and produce a harvest of unifying pleasure for your family.

35 FAMILY IDEAS

1. Have an indoor picnic.

2. Plant a family tree together.

3. Plan a family slumber party.

4. Record family songs or skits on a blank tape or video cassette.

5. Take a "dream" vacation with the family. Get travel brochures and library books about places you'd like to visit. Everyone take turns sharing his idea of the best vacation.

6. Make homemade ice cream together or create an original cookie recipe.

7. Let everyone share his favorite music for a music appreciation night.

8. Encourage everyone to share the truth in love and have a family gripe time to air out feelings and repair broken relationships.

9. If grandparents don't live close by, take children to a nursing home to adopt a grandparent.

10. Have family devotions; read the Bible, pray together, sing hymns.

11. The next time it rains, have everyone take a walk together without umbrellas.

12. Take a camera and roll of film to the park to shoot a roll of family pictures.

13. Have the family rearrange the picture albums, add pictures, and write captions under pictures.

14. Read a book together. Read a chapter each night.

15. Try round-robin story telling. Sit in a circle and have

someone start telling a made-up story. When he reaches an exciting part, he stops and someone else continues.

16. Have a family car wash. Ending with a water fight is always fun.

17. Spend an evening watching family movies and eating popcorn.

18. A great way to send a letter to relatives is to have each person in the family begin a letter (little ones can draw). After a few minutes everyone switches letters and continues writing on the new letter, and so on, until everyone has written on each letter.

19. Celebrate a season swap day. In the winter have an indoor summer picnic, and in the summer build a small fire and drink hot chocolate.

20. Turn the kids into reporters to find out family history from relatives; then make a family tree together.

21. Once school is out, mark a family calendar with dates of family excursions, places to visit together, books to read, or hobbies to work on.

22. Encourage the family to write notes to each other on a large family blackboard.

23. Mothers and fathers should make periodic "dates" with young sons and daughters.

24. Change one of your house rules for an evening, such as "no roughhousing" or "no food in the living room." Let small children know you can break the rules and have fun when the rules are followed the rest of the time.

25. Let little ones participate in your garage sale and reap profits from their own sale of toys or cookies.

26. Play games together as a family. Many adult games can have rules adapted for children.

27. Play "balloon volleyball" in the house with the adults on their knees.

28. Invent a holiday to celebrate—Teddy Bear Day, Pizza Day, etc.

29. Make up a family trivia game with questions about family dates of importance, places the family has been, relatives, funny memories, etc.

30. Plan a family scavenger hunt or clue hunt with a family treat as the treasure.

31. Birthdays can be extra special without added cost by giving the person a "birthday week." During the week of the birthday, other family members give him special attention and give him first choice in small family decisions.

32. One of the best all-time gifts family members can give to each other for any occasion is "coupons." Decorate a card and write on it a promise of time or work for the person you are giving it to. For example, "This entitles you to one evening free of dishes." "Saturday morning goof-off coupon." Younger children can draw pictures of what they will do, such as clean out the car, or share a toy.

V-18

33. Each year for Christmas, shop as a family for one special tree ornament.

34. On Christmas Eve, write down everyone's predictions for the family during the next year. Seal them and pack them away with the Christmas decorations to be read next Christmas Eve.

35. To overcome the "after-Christmas blues," start a tradition of starting a family jigsaw puzzle the day after Christmas.

SUMMARY

All it takes for a woman to excel at housekeeping is a little know-how, daily prayer, and some imagination. A home is a place you want to spend all your time. A mother is the one who makes it that way. As you apply Bible principles to housekeeping you'll grow as a Noble Woman. Think of your family as a small church body. Everyone must do his part or the whole body suffers. Keep your family informed about your housekeeping and delegate duties to each of them. Be warm and loving with your family. Create family traditions you can build on. Share your family life with others. God has given a noble responsibility to women in the home.

ASSIGNMENT

Memorize Proverbs 3:33-35. How appropriate to learn the words found in verse 33, "...he blesses the home of the righteous." Congratulations on having memorized two complete chapters in the Bible. You should be convinced of your memory abilities and eager to continue memorizing and reviewing Scripture.

Suggestion: "But the seed on good soil stands for those with a noble and good heart, who hear the word, retain it, and by persevering produce a crop" (Luke 8:15). Think of a crop of corn. One seed bears a plant with four or five ears of corn, each with hundreds of similar seeds. Once you've memorized Scripture, produce a crop by sharing memory verses hundreds of times with others. Each time you share your verses, you'll reproduce that seed within yourself.

Lesson 19
Relationships

V-19

PURPOSE
To learn how to improve your relationships.

OVERVIEW
Christianity is based on relationships. You have a relationship with your Lord. How you treat that relationship affects your life in vital proportions. You have a relationship to other Christians. *"We know that we have passed from death to life, because we love our brothers"* (I John 3:14). How you treat others is God's rule of meausre (Matthew 7:1-2). You have a relationship to the world. *"Though I am free and belong to no man, I make myself a slave to everyone, to win as many as possible"* (I Corinthians 9:19). You have a relationship with spouse and child, parent, and sibling. You have relationships with those you choose — your friends.

DISCUSSION
Relationships should be founded on love. *"Above all, love each other deeply, because love covers over a multitude of sins"* (I Peter 4:8). Love is an elusive quality. It can be a noun, a verb, an adjective, an emotion, a cause or an effect. Love can give new meaning to a mundane task. It can elevate the simple to the sublime, the ordinary to the meaningful. *"And let us consider how we may spur one another on toward love and good deeds"* (Hebrews 10:24). Love is a command of God. You must find a way to attain it. *"Dear friends, let us love one another, for love comes from God"* (I John 4:7). How do you develop relationships built on love? Only with the help of God. He's always willing for you to love. His capacity for loving relationships is great; He wants yours to be too. He doesn't want you to neglect certain kinds of relationships and favor others. He wants you to love everyone. In His Word He teaches how to build each kind of relationship.

Relationships God Wants You to Develop:

1. **You and Jesus.** In the gospel written by John, the author refers to himself as "the disciple whom Jesus loved." John's relationship was special to Jesus because John chose to press in close to Him. John was always mentioned as being near or with Jesus. Often Jesus would leave His followers and take the twelve disciples to be with Him privately. Sometimes He would leave nine disciples and take Peter, James, and John. But John was the one called "the disciple who Jesus loved." Why was John so favored? Did he have a special quality the others didn't? No, anyone could have taken John's place. He was favored by Jesus because he pressed in and made himself available to Jesus.

John's gospel is written from a relationship perspective. It shows the relationship between Jesus and His father, and Jesus and His disciples (John 15 and 16). The emotional scene of the last supper is recorded in more detail in the Book of John. It's from his viewpoint that John 13 says, *"Having loved his own who were in the world, he now showed them the full extent of his love."* John sat next to Jesus during the Last Supper. John was the first to recognize Jesus on the shore after the resurrection. He reveals his immense love for Jesus in the last verse of the Gospel of John: *"Jesus did many other things as well. If every one of them were written down, I suppose that even the whole world would not have room for the books that would be written."* John truly knew Jesus.

Even after Jesus returned to heaven, John's behavior was directed by his love for Jesus. He reached Him in the Spirit when he could no longer reach Him in the flesh. On the island of Patmos John saw the vision which he gave in the Book of Revelation. John was allowed a fuller glimpse of heaven than anyone else because he bonded himself to Jesus in a strong relationship built on love.

This kind of relationship with Jesus is yours for the asking. Because John pursued Jesus he was able to claim Him as a close friend. Pursue Jesus and He will offer the same kind of relationship to you.

2. **You and other Christians.** As two strong believers, Mary and Elizabeth portray the kind of sweet and encouraging relationship Christians should have with each other. Both women were sensitive to what God wanted for their lives. Elizabeth welcomed Mary into her home with gladness and didn't worry about how the neighbors would feel about an unwed mother. But Elizabeth also didn't smother Mary with undue attention. She gave motherly concern and respect at the same time. The women didn't make demands on each other but were sensitive to each other's needs. From the very beginning of their time of fellowship, found in Luke 1:39-56, these women understood the importance of centering their relationship on God (Luke 1:44).

When given an opportunity to spend time together, these two Godly women enriched their lives by openly relating to each other. The Bible doesn't say if Mary and Elizabeth were accustomed to seeing each other before this three-month visit. What is known is that they both responded lovingly to God's arranging to bring their lives together. You should be willing in your life to let God direct your relationships with other Christians. When an opportunity presents itself to spend time with another Christian, make yourself available to enrich his life. Center your relationship on Jesus.

3. **You and non-Christians.** A Christian's relationship with a non-Christian is important to God. *"As for the foreigner who does not belong to your people Israel, but has come from a distant land because of your great name and your mighty hand and your out- stretched arm — when he comes and prays toward this temple, then hear from heaven, your dwelling place, and do whatever the foreigner asks of you"* (I Kings 8:41-43). King Solomon, the wisest man in the world, knew to be gracious to nonbelievers. The Temple was designed with an outer court where foreigners could come and worship God, too. God always makes room for the nonbeliever;

you should too. God knew from the beginning, people would be attracted to His Kingdom. He has always made loving provision for them to come into His fold. It's important to accept sinners as they are when they first attend church services or come into your home. It's the Holy Spirit that does a changing work in their lives *after* they've been born again. You must be patient to see these visible changes from sinner to saint.

Learn to look at non-Christians through the eyes of Jesus and show them His hospitality. You may be criticized as Jesus was in Matthew 9:11-12, *"On hearing this, Jesus said, 'It is not the healthy who need a doctor, but the sick.'"* Your attitude toward non-Christians should be that of a servant bringing Jesus to them to meet their needs. Paul said it best in I Corinthians 9:19: *"Though I am free and belong to no man, I make myself a slave to everyone, to win as many as possible."*

V-19

4. **You and your spouse.** God has much to say about the marriage relationship. After all, the mystery of the Church is that marriage represents Christ and the Church. It's an important institution to God and shouldn't be regarded lightly. The first miracle performed by Jesus was at a wedding. Jesus wants marriages to survive. *"Anyone who divorces his wife and marries another woman commits adultery against her. And if she divorces her husband and marries another man, she commits adultery"* (Mark 10:11-12). God joins the husband and wife together as one. The commands for husbands to love their wives and wives to submit to their husbands in Ephesians 5 are unconditional.

5. **You and your child.** Many Christian women get their priorities out of line when they put the mother/child relationship above the wife/husband relationship. This error can also be witnessed in Scripture with disasterous results. When Rebekah favored her son, Jacob's wishes over her husband's, she brought trouble into the family situation and caused Jacob to be banished from home. On the other hand, Abraham dearly loved his son Isaac, but was willing to give him to God, and to regard his wife's needs before his children's. This should be your relationship with your children. Train them up in God's ways, and let God have them. It's easy for mothers to fall into Rebekah's pattern and try to manage their chidlren's futures; to want to keep them from making their own mistakes. This over-protection and maneuvering doesn't prepare them to be men and women of God, though. You must love them dearly while giving them over to God. You must listen to your spouse's needs above the desires of your children.

6. **You and your parents.** You aren't excluded from honoring your parents when you reach adulthood. Being ungrateful and disobedient to your parents is a sign of humanism (II Timothy 3:2). If one of your parents dies, it's your responsibility to care for the surviving parent. *"But if a widow has children or grandchildren, these should learn first of all to put their religion into practice by caring for their own family and so repaying their parents and grandparents, for this is pleasing to God"* (I Timothy 5:4.)

7. **You and your Christian friends.** No one could be a greater model of Christian friendship in the Bible than Paul. His letters

constantly allude to his numerous deep relationships with fellow Christians. He must have learned the Godly concepts of quantity and quality time. God provided ample opportunity for Paul to build friendships. These friends emotionally and prayerfully carried Paul through his worst physical times, and the difficulties he endured during the last years of his life.

Paul didn't let traveling persuade him to forgo friendship. Even though he would establish a church and then move on, he made the effort to form friendships. He would keep in contact through letters and visits. He combined ministry and friendship by taking Silas and Timothy on his missionary travels. When in prison Paul writes to Timothy: *"I long to see you, so that I may be filled with joy"* (II Timothy 1:4). Paul was never ashamed to share his true feelings with his friends. Cultivate strong Christian friendships with a sense of trust and help in time of crisis. Reveal your true feelings for your friends, spending enough quantity time to establish the relationship and adding enough quality time, periodically, to help the relationship grow.

What Can Affect a Relationship?

1. **Time.** There's a misconception that quality time makes up for quantity. You can't achieve true quality time unless you have a previous record of quantity time. It takes time for people to get to know each other well enough to be considered friends, close friends, or intimate friends. Layers of your personality are cautiously folded back to reveal the true person hiding behind opinions, likes and dislikes, and even Christian doctrine. You can't just call up a casual friend and propose to engage in quality time to further your relationship. This is because quality time is birthed from quantity.

If you spend enough time with a casual friend finding mutual interests and discovering shared concerns, you realize that during the quantity time together, quality time was born. After you spend time discovering the preliminaries (childhood, religious background, inner desires, admired qualities, character strengths and weaknesses, personal opinions), the intimacy and fellowship process develops quickly enough that spending a lot of time together isn't nearly as important as spending some time. You replace quantity time with quality time. Intimate friends don't doubt your desire to be with them, so demand less time; but this isn't always so. Sooner or later friends, even intimate ones, will become suspicious of your true feelings if you neglect them. Sometimes spending hours doing nothing in particular means more than only being around for the important occasions.

How do you apply this to family situations? Again, you must give a spouse and children the feeling you enjoy spending your time with them. Quantity time breeds quality. Both are necessary. The family vacation is an example. The idea that a family could go through a year without any planned activities together and expect to have fun and relaxation spending a week or two with only each other is a mistake. Family members must spend enough time learning how to "be" together before they can spend time having fun and relaxing together. Don't forget the notion of quality time, just be sure there's enough quantity time to support it.

2. The tongue. Nothing can damage a relationship faster than saying the wrong thing at the wrong time. *"My dear brothers, take note of this: Everyone should be quick to listen, slow to speak and slow to become angry"* (James 1:19). Everything you say to friends and family can be placed in one of two categories—words that build, or words that damage a relationship. It's not always *what* you say that matters, but *how* you say it. Many wise verses in Proverbs advise wives not to quarrel with their husbands. This is an area in which the devil strongly attacks women. *"What causes fights and quarrels among you?"* (James 4:1) The tongue can do much damage in the home. Strive to be the peacemaker among family members; speak encouraging words to your family. *"But the wisdom that comes from heaven is first of all pure; then peace loving, considerate, submissive, full of mercy and good fruit, impartial, and sincere"* (James 3:17).

3. Friendship. Are you a good friend or a bad friend? The kind of friend you are affects your relationships. Learn the qualities of a good friend from the Bible. *"Greater love has no one than this, that one lay down his life for his friends"* (John 15:13). A true friend is one who will always stay a friend, always show love (Proverbs 17:17, 18:24, 27:10).

"The pleasantness of one's friend springs from his earnest counsel" (Proverbs 27:9). Besides sharing honest counsel, a good friend shares good news (Mark 5:19, Luke 15:6) and good times (Luke 14:10-12). Jesus was a friend to those who needed Him. (Matthew 11:19). A good friend will be patient, kind, protective, trusting, and never failing in a relationship (I Corinthians 13:4-8).

4. The power of God. Finally, in building relationships with friends and family, be assured God has given you everything you need (II Peter 1:3). In II Peter 1:5-7, God gives the secret to building relationships. It is the principle of "adding to" what you have in each relationship. *"For this very reason, make every effort to add to your faith goodness; and to goodness, knowledge; and to knowledge, self-control; and to self-control, perseverance; and to perseverance, godliness; and to godliness, brotherly kindess; and to brotherly kindness, love."* Relationships grow gradually, measure by measure. In a relationship, start by having faith in someone; then begin to establish the friendship by doing something good for the person. Fellowship further by informing each other about yourselves. Control your tongue by listening well and saying only good things. Next, persevere in finding quantity and quality time to spend together. As your relationship grows, you should inspire godliness in each other. Finally, aspire to brotherly kindness and love.

SUMMARY

Relationships make life meaningful. God wants you to build your relationship with Him, family, friends, non-Christians, and Christians. To do that you must spend time, quantity and quality, with people. You must display self-control and guard your tongue. Be a good friend. Say good things to your friends; praise their Bible-based opinions, and speak highly of them to others. Use your tongue to affect your relationships in a positive way.

Think only the best of your friends and family. Invite the power of God to work in your life and "add to" each of your relationships until they all have goodness, knowledge, self-control, perseverance, godliness, brotherly kindness, and love.

ASSIGNMENT

Now that you've memorized two chapters from the Bible, this assignment will appear easy. Memorize Philippians 4:8 to remind yourself of the proper attitude to have when building relationships.

Suggestion: Your body responds to cues that are consistent and reinforcing. Memorize Scripture at the same time, and same place each day. You'll find it easier to memorize.

TABLE 8
KINDS OF LOVE

1. THE LOVE OF GOD

    II Corinthians 2:4
    II Corinthians 5:14
    II Corinthians 13:11

2. PERFECT LOVE

    I John 4:8
    I John 4:17,18
    Ephesians 3:19

3. BROTHERLY LOVE

    Philippians 1:9
    Colossians 1:4
    II Timothy 1:7

4. GIVING LOVE

    Galatians 5:6
    Galatians 5:13
    Hebrews 13:1

Lesson 20
The End of a Thing

V-20

PURPOSE

To achieve the end of the difficult journey of becoming a Noble Woman. To perfect the finer points of being a Noble Woman.

OVERVIEW

"Many women do noble things, but you surpass them all" (Proverbs 31:29). Congratulations for discovering the secrets to becoming a Noble Woman, applying them to your own life, and reaching the end of your journey. Though you will never reach perfection until heaven (I Corinthians 15:53), you can live the life of a Noble Woman. As you approach the end of discovering Noble Womanhood, revive your spirit with fresh insights into God's Word.

This lesson discusses difficult aspects of being a Christian. You'll study passages in the Bible you wish weren't there — the ones that seem too hard to obey. However, God gives you the power to do all that He asks. Plant the seeds of true Christianity deep in your heart for a fruitful harvest.

DISCUSSION

There are certain requirements God places on the spiritual Christian. The carnal Christian is led by his fleshly desires, but the spiritual Christian must follow the leading of the Holy Spirit down the path of unselfishness. Certainly a Noble Woman should be a spiritual Christian. Scripture warns that once you've tasted of the milk of God's Word, you need to move on to the meat (Hebrews 6:1-3). As you've developed in the four areas of growth and achieve the balance of a Noble Woman, you've fed on the milk of the Bible. Now you should be ready for the meat.

There are commands given by God throughout the Bible that only Christians walking in the Spirit truly hear. Does your spirit quicken at these verses? Then God has called you to fulfill His commands.

Giving:

1. **Give to the poor.** *"If there is a poor man among your brothers in any of the towns of the land that the Lord your God is giving you, do not be hardhearted or tightfisted toward your poor brother. Rather be openhanded and freely lend him whatever he needs"* (Deuteronomy 15:7-8), *"There will always be poor people in the land. Therefore I command you to be openhanded toward your brothers and toward the poor and needy in your land"* (Deuteronomy 15:11). Giving to an organization that provides for the poor, instead of directly to a

147

poor family, may not have the same result. The Noble Woman in Proverbs 31 gave to the poor directly from her door. There is something about looking into the very eyes of a poor person and meeting a specific need that makes you see yourself in the light of truth. Another man's want makes your own blessings more evident. This doesn't mean you should exclude yourself from any luxuries you might be able to afford. Jesus said there will always be poor people (Mark 14:7). You're only asked to be willing to help any who come into your life needing help. Don't ignore the poor. There's always someone worse off than your own family.

Another factor in giving to someone in need is to give more than is asked of you. *"And if someone wants to sue you and take your tunic, let him have your cloak as well. If someone forces you to go one mile, go with him two miles. Give to the one who asks you, and do not turn away from the one who wants to borrow from you"* (Matthew 5:40-42). What's the biggest fear in fulfilling this request from God? Do you think if you give to everyone who asks there will be nothing left for yourself, that you'll be taken advantage of? God is keeping a heavenly record. He promises to pay you back (Proverbs 28:27). You can't outgive God. He always has a way of returning blessings to you. The hard truth is you *must* give to the poor. *"If anyone has material possession and sees his brother in need but has no pity on him, how can the love of God be in him?"* (I John 3:17). The reality of your Christianity rides on whether you give to the poor.

2. **Care for strangers.** *"Do not forget to entertain strangers"* (Hebrews 13:2). This is stressful in an age when criminals act in the light of day and terrorize even those who are kind to them; but the words of God still hold true. *"If anyone gives a cup of cold water to one of these little ones because he is my disciple, I tell you the truth, he will certainly not lose his reward"* (Matthew 10:42). If you're sensitive to the Holy Spirit, you'll be directed to which strangers God wants you to care for. While the rest of the world forgets the stranger wandering on the streets, loitering at shopping centers, or asking for help, make a point of helping strangers throughout your life.

3. **Visit the sick.** *"When did we see you sick or in prison and go to visit you? The King will reply, 'I tell you the truth, whatever you did for one of the least of these brothers of mine, you did for me.'"* (Matthew 25:39-40). This includes the elderly, the invalid, and those in your church congregation who get sick. Of course you're to pray for the sick that they may recover, but until their recovery is complete you should give the gift of time to those who need care. The sick usually feel the world is passing them by. When you break out of the busyness of your world to spend time with the sick, you give joy and life that helps the sick person get well.

4. **Help someone in prison.** Read Matthew 25:31-46. Here prisoners are categorized as needy, along with the poor and sick. Why did God do that? People tend to think that prisoners deserve their fate, and therefore, aren't worthy of attention. God knows there are some innocent and unfortunate people in prison, even the guilty can be repentant and in need of compassion. Although prisoners tend to become "out of sight and out of

mind" God doesn't want you to forget them; they're the needy, too.

Think of juvenile delinquents you migh influence by showering them with the loving attention they crave. Think of the adults, deceived into following the evil of the world, you could touch with God's love. Many Christian prison ministries today need help. Men and women in prison are a natural audience to hear of the saving grace of Jesus Christ. They know better than anyone this world doesn't have much to offer. They need Jesus, and they need someone to care. Jesus wants that someone to be you.

5. **Don't be a shallow Christian.** Give your thought life to God. Do you know that every idle thought and word you speak is recorded by God and will one day be judged by Him? *"So then, each of us will give an account of himself to God"* (Romans 14:12). Jesus made it plain during the Sermon on the Mount that you not only shouldn't sin, but shouldn't even entertain the thought of sinning. Each person is responsible for his true self, his thought life. God can look into your soul and spirit to see what your motives are for not sinning. Having the appearance of being spiritual is easy; having the desire to really please God is another matter. *"If any man builds on this foundation using gold, silver, costly stones, wood, hay or straw, his work will be shown for what it is, because the Day will bring it to light. It will be revealed with fire, and the fire will test the quality of each man's work. If what he has built survives, he will receive his reward. If it is burned up, he will suffer loss; he himself will be saved, but only as one escaping through the flames"* (I Corinthians 3:12-15).

6. **Use your talents for God** (Proverbs 16:3). *"Each one should use whatever gift he has received to serve others, faithfully administering God's grace in its various forms"* (I Peter 4:10). *"His master replied, 'Well done, good and faithful servant! You have been faithful with a few things; I will put you in charge of many things. Come and share your master's happiness!'"* (Matthew 25:23). In being accountable for your actions, be accountable for using your talents. Don't let your life be wasted on earthly goals that will be gone like a vapor when your earthly life is over. Do you want to succeed with your talent? Do you want to have a lasting impact with your life? (Proverbs 16:3).

7. **Follow Jesus' example of selflessness.** The hardest life to live is one lived for no one but yourself. *"Then Jesus said to his disciples, 'If anyone would come after me, he must deny himself and take up his cross and follow me. For whoever wants to save his life will lose it, but whoever loses his life for me will find it'"* (Matthew 16:24-25). Once you've learned to give up your rights to fill the needs of others, you'll discover the joy of a life of love. You'll feel God's face shine upon you with pleasure and you'll know you've gained what's important on earth and in heaven.

Learn not to question God. Don't blame Him for the sorrow in your life. Don't demand explanation from Him. Everyone reaches times when compelled to ask, "Why?" When you need comfort in suffering, turn from yourself to God's Word. *"In this you greatly rejoice, though now for a little while you may have had to suffer grief in all kinds of trials. These have come so that your faith — of greater worth than gold, which perishes even though refined by fire — may be proved genuine and may result in praise, glory and honor when Jesus Christ is revealed"* (I Peter 1:6-7). *"Dear friends, do not be surprised at the painful trial you are suffering, as though something strange were happening to you"* (I Peter 4:12). A life of selflessness has pain, but it also has joy.

8. **Realize that, to God, one sin is as bad as another.** There is no degree of sin in God's mind. For instance, it's easy to indulge in the sin of murmuring. Yet this sin is as evil to God as performing witchcraft. (I Samuel 15:23). Don't fool yourself into thinking little sins are alright with God. He wants you to be as holy and pure as He is.

9. **Don't fall into the trap of judgment.** There's a fine line between keeping yourself from the world and the influence of carnal Christians and making the mistake of judging your brothers and neighbors. Only God knows a person's heart. He's interested in motives, not actions. *"Do not judge, or you too will be judged . . . Why do you look at the speck of sawdust in your brother's eye and pay no attention to the plank in your own eye?"* (Matthew 7:1 and 3). Instead of judging, check your own heart for sin, jealousy, lack of love, or ignorance. Loving your neighbor means assuming the best and accepting actions as well intentioned. Even people you would normally hate or consider enemies, should be treated without judgment. This is an instance when mercy is a virtue. God has actually said to love those who persecute you. Anyone can love those who love him; a real test of spirituality is loving someone who doesn't love you (Matthew 5:43-48).

10. **The ultimate spiritual goal is revealed in James 1:27.** *"Religion that God our Father accepts as pure and faultless is this: to look after orphans and widows in their distress and to keep oneself from being polluted by the world."* Do you know of any widows or orphaned children? Consider children of divorced parents fatherless as well. Are you helping to meet their needs?

Receiving:

Most Christians understand the principle of giving. They know even if it's difficult, it's important for them to give to others. Moreover, some Christians never have a difficult time giving. Their generous spirit is always witnessed in the offering plate or when the restaurant check is picked up. These Christians are the first to help out in their children's schools, or make cookies for a club, or make a donation to a worthy cause. But for these Christians there's another area of weakness God may want them to experience and learn from—the area of receiving. While a giver can be bold or shy, a receiver must be gracious and thankful.

God intends us to have times of need in our lives. *"Do not be like them, for your Father knows what you need before you ask him"* (Matthew 6:8). He intends for you to go to fellow Christians when you have a need. This is what the early Church did. *"All the believers were together and had everything in common. Selling their possessions and goods, they gave to anyone as he had need."* (Acts 2:44-45). They weren't embarrassed to give or receive. Without a need to receive during some time in our lives, we wouldn't have God-pleasing faith. *"And without faith it is impossible to please God"* (Hebrews 11:6).

A receiver is used of God to enable another person to be blessed of God. In this way, the one who gives receives a blessing from the Lord, and the one who receives is blessed by the giver. Always being the giver and never the receiver opens the door to the sin of pride. Being the receiver is a humbling experience. How many of us go looking for humbling experiences?

Receiving someone's help means you have to be vulnerable. You have to admit you have a need, which often gets translated as a fault. But you can't fulfill the law of Christ unless you share your burdens (Galatians 6:2). Christians must tell each other when there is a need. Whether it's a need for a compliment, companionship, money, food, clothing, shelter, or love, you must allow others in God's family to meet your need. Often God allows you to be in need so another Christian will give to you. It's the way God's system works; it's the way a family works.

A Noble Woman often has the most difficult time receiving. Her life revolves around giving. She gives encouragement to her husband; she fills the needs of a smooth-running household; she nurtures her children from conception on; she gives to the poor, to the church, to her friends, and to herself by taking care of her physical needs.

She's a seemingly endless supply of giving. But again, if she doesn't allow herself to also receive, she can fall prey to the dangerous sin of pride. She'll think of herself as Supermom, Superwife, Superwoman. God wants you to learn grace and mercy through receiving. *"Dear friends, do not be surprised at the painful trial you are suffering, as though something strange were happening to you. But rejoice that you participate in the sufferings of Christ, so that you may be overjoyed when his glory is revealed'* (I Peter 4:12-13).

A Noble Woman needs to receive from her husband, even if it's a simple compliment. When she's worked hard to clean, organize, or prepare a wonderful meal she should reveal her need for appreciation. She should let her husband and children know when she needs physical help in the household. She should let her friends know when she needs friendship. When her family is suffering she should be willing to accept love gifts of time, food, money, or help from others. Sometimes when God begins to work through others (how else can He work?) in giving to you, receiving so much love and attention in a time of need can be overwhelming. Learn to accept and receive graciously. Follow these guidelines:

1. **Never turn down someone's gift** (even if you feel your need isn't great enough for the gift). This is the ultimate rejection of the giver. God has opened someone's heart to give; receive as though it were from God, who will always give more than you expect. *"Now to him who is able to do immeasurably more than we ask or imagine, according to his power that is at work within us"* (Ephesians 3:20).

2. **Be truthful about a need.** If a giver of food asks you what you need, don't suggest beans and cornbread if your family never eats it. Don't lie and say everything is fine and you have plenty if you don't. *"Ask and it will be given to you; seek and you will find; knock and the door will be opened to you. For everyone who asks receives; he who seeks finds; and to him who knocks, the door will be opened. Which of you, if his son asks for bread, will give him a stone? Or if he asks for a fish, will give him a snake? If you, then, though you are evil, know how to give good gifts to your children, how much more will your Father in heaven give good gifts to those who ask him!"* (Matthew 7:7-11).

3. **Say a simple thank you.** Trying to match a gift with equal thanks or appreciation only complicates the giving for the giver. Let God bless the giver. You are not responsible for "paying back" a gift. *"Every good and perfect gift is from above, coming down from the Father"* (James 1:17). Let the giver know that God will bless him and you are glad, since he will be able to pay back better than you could. Tell the giver you hope one day you will be able to help someone in just the same way and their kindness will again be remembered. Let the giver know you'll pray for him. Let the giver know the gift will go directly to the need. (For example, if the money was for food, let the giver know when you're going to the store.)

God wants you to give as He gives, but He also wants you to receive from Him, as a child taking pleasure in the love gifts God provides through others. Read the following verse with the emphasis on receiving. *"Give and it shall be **given to you**. A good measure, pressed down, shaken together and running over, **will** men give unto you"* (Luke 6:38 KJV).

Life in the Spirit:

Listen to what the Spirit of God tells you. If Christians are going to be the Church, without spot or wrinkle, that Jesus is returning for (II Peter 3:14), we must commit ourselves to the task of submitting always to the Holy Spirit. Live by your spiritual sense. All kinds of emotions and actions can be done in the Spirit. Here are a few you might not be aware of:

1. *"Watch and pray so that you will not fall into temptation. The spirit is willing but the body is weak"* (Matthew 26:41). Man's spirit displays emotions and will, separate from and sometimes in conflict with, the soul. Listen to the desires of your spirit over the desires of your flesh.

2. *"Immediately Jesus knew in his spirit that this was what they were thinking in their hearts"* (Mark 2:8). Your spirit can perceive things your mind doesn't know.

3. *"At that time Jesus, full of joy through the Holy Spirit . . ."* (Luke 10:21). The spirit can feel intense emotion.

4. *"Yet a time is coming and has now come when the true worshippers will worship the Father in spirit and truth, for they are the kind of worshippers the Father seeks"* (John 4:23). Let your spirit worship God. It's the only way we can "feel" His presence.

5. *"He was deeply moved in spirit and troubled"* (John 11:33). Your

spirit can let you know when something is amiss, when temptation to sin is near. The wise Christian will pay attention when his spirit is troubled.

6. *"And now, compelled by the Spirit, I am going to Jerusalem"* (Acts 20:22). When God's direction is extremely important, His Holy Spirit communicates to your spirit with strong urgings.

7. *"For who among men knows the thoughts of a man except the man's spirit within him?"* (I Corinthians 2:11) Your spirit knows your true self; trust it.

8. *"But by faith we eagerly await through the Spirit the righteousness for which we hope"* (Galatians 5:5). Waiting on God is nearly impossible in the flesh; let your spirit handle the waiting.

9. *"The one who sows to please his sinful nature, from that nature will reap destruction; the one who sows to please the Spirit, from the Spirit will reap eternal life"* (Galatians 6:8). The spirit of man sows and reaps spiritually, even as man's soul sows and reaps. Eternal life is returned in many ways—life with God, blessing, and spiritual authority over powers of evil.

10. *"And pray in the Spirit on all occasions with all kinds of prayers and requests"* (Ephesians 6:18). Pray in the spirit to make your prayers more effective.

11. *"And who also told us of your love in the Spirit"* (Colossians 1:8). Loving in the spirit is the highest form of love.

Pulling it All Together

"The end of a matter is better than its beginning" (Ecclesiastes 7:8). You've learned the value of wisdom and how to obtain it. You understand the elements of growing in stature. You know the importance of rest without worry, hard work, and food eaten with thanksgiving. You've grown in favor with God by developing your personal relationship with Jesus, by setting aside time to spend with Him, and by praying. Becoming a Noble Woman you've gained the favor of family, friends, fellow Christians, and have become a witness to non-Christians. You've examined all four areas of growth and have learned to balance them. Whenever your life appears out of balance, simply examine area again to identify the problem. One way to keep track of your noble efforts is to record your life in a journal. Write down your thoughts, your desires, your discoveries in Scripture, and the pattern of your daily life.

SUMMARY

Being a Christian (or Christ one) is the act of patterning your life after Jesus Christ. As Jesus grew in wisdom, stature, and in favor of God and men, so must you. The woman in Proverbs 31 was noble, excellent in all she did. She performed mentally, physically, spiritually, and socially in such a way that she became God's ideal woman. The qualities of Noble Womanhood are attainable. They may require sacrifice on your part, but the benefits are worth it. Living your life as a Noble Woman is like the parable of the pearl of great price. *"Again, the kingdom of* heaven is like a merchant looking for fine pearls. When he found one of great value, he went away and sold everything he had and bought it" (Matthew 13:45-46).

Give up your life to acquire the noble life God has for you. Build up yourself and others. Listen to the Holy Spirit and seek after wisdom. "Jesus replied; 'Love the Lord your God with all your heart and with all your soul and with all your mind. This is the first and greatest commandment. And the second is like it: Love your neighbor as yourself'"(Matthew 22:37-39).

ASSIGNMENT

"Jesus told him, 'Go and do likewise'" (Luke 10:37). Do you hear Jesus telling you this today? Your assignment is to go and do what Jesus did — grow in wisdom, stature, and favor with God and men for the rest of your life.

Suggestion: The best suggestion at this point is for you to realize the Holy Spirit will do the work of a Noble Woman within you if you let Him. "Not by might nor by power, but by my Spirit, says the Lord Almighty" (Zechariah 4:6).